2 Samuel

Verse By Verse Ministry International

Taught by
Stephen Armstrong and Wesley Livingston

Copyright © 2024 by **Verse By Verse Ministry International**

All rights reserved. No part of this publication may be reproduced, distributed, or transmitted in any form or by any means, without prior written permission.

Unless otherwise noted, all Scripture quotations are taken from the New American Standard Bible® (NASB1995), copyright © 1960, 1962, 1963, 1968, 1971, 1972, 1973, 1975, 1977, 1995 by The Lockman Foundation. Used by permission. All rights reserved. Lockman.org.

Scripture quotations marked (KJV) are taken from the King James Bible. Accessed on Bible Gateway. www.BibleGateway.com.

Renown Publishing
www.renownpublishing.com

2 Samuel / Verse By Verse Ministry International
ISBN-13: 978-1-960236-20-3

To those with eyes for eternity—

Pursue the study of Scripture with zeal, as it produces a great intimacy with Christ.

May God open your eyes to the glory of His grace and truth.

CONTENTS

GETTING STARTED v
DAVID MOURNS SAUL'S DEATH: CHAPTER 1 9
DIVIDED KINGDOM, DIVIDED HEART: CHAPTERS 2:1–32 & 3:1–16 19
DAVID'S OBSTACLES FALL: CHAPTERS 3:17–39; 4; & 5:1–5 33
WALKING IN THE WILL OF GOD: CHAPTER 5 & 6:1–5 43
TRUE WORSHIP IS OBEDIENCE: CHAPTERS 6:6–23 & 7:1–16 53
AWAITING A PROMISED KINGDOM: CHAPTER 7 65
A GOD WHO KEEPS LOVINGKINDNESS: CHAPTERS 8 & 9 73
A CORRUPTED HEART: CHAPTERS 10 & 11 83
SIN EXPOSED: CHAPTER 12 95
THE CONSEQUENCES OF DAVID'S SIN: CHAPTER 13:1–22 103
SYSTEMIC ISSUES IN DAVID'S FAMILY: CHAPTER 14 115
DAVID'S FLIGHT: CHAPTERS 14:28–33 & 15 125
DAVID'S FLIGHT, CONTINUED: CHAPTERS 16 & 17 135
THE DOWNFALL OF ABSALOM: CHAPTERS 17:24–29; 18; & 19:1–7 147
REINSTATED AS KING: CHAPTER 19 159
SHEBA'S REBELLION: CHAPTER 20 169
BIBLICAL JUSTICE: CHAPTER 21:1–14 179
"THE HORN OF MY SALVATION": CHAPTERS 21:15–22 & 22:1–20 187
DAVID'S PRAISE TO THE LORD: CHAPTER 22:20–51 195
DAVID'S LAST SONG: CHAPTER 23:1–7 205
THE REWARD OF GREAT MEN: CHAPTER 23:8–39 213
SIN, JUDGMENT, AND RESTORATION: CHAPTER 24 223
ANSWER KEY 233
ABOUT THE AUTHORS 319

INTRODUCTION

Getting Started

The purpose of this introduction is to orient you to our study before we begin the sessions. To start, here are some guidelines to help you read and interpret God's word.

Two Rules for Interpretation

The Golden Rule (of Scripture interpretation): When the plain sense of the text makes common sense, seek no further sense.

Also, remember that symbols will always be interpreted by Scripture itself. You never have to guess. As you go through this study, find hope and reassurance in knowing that God wants you to understand His word.

Session Overview

Here is an overview of some sections you will encounter in each session of this study:

- Topic Overview
- Learning Goals
- Core Questions
- Discussion Questions
- Digging Deeper
- A Little Deeper

ABOUT "DIGGING DEEPER" AND "A LITTLE DEEPER"

Between sessions, you will have the opportunity to complete "Digging Deeper" and "A Little Deeper" sections that will help you delve further into the topics covered in the teaching while also preparing for the next session. Each meeting will open with a discussion of what you have observed in and learned from Scripture.

To record what you observe in each passage and the questions you have about it, use the lined note-taking spaces provided for observations and questions (see below).

Things to look for:

- Who is speaking?
- To whom is he speaking?
- What does this passage say about God, about Jesus, about the church, and about individual believers?
- What do readers of this text stand to gain?

OBSERVATIONS

_____
_____
_____
_____
_____
_____
_____
_____
_____
_____
_____
_____

QUESTIONS

2 Samuel

SESSION 1

David Mourns Saul's Death: Chapter 1

Read 2 Samuel 1:1–27.

TOPIC OVERVIEW

- Author and background of 1–2 Samuel
- Significance of key players and events surrounding Saul's death
- David's mourning

LEARNING GOALS

- Determine major themes throughout the chapter.
- Identify events in David's life in which God's sovereignty can be clearly seen.

CORE QUESTIONS

Answer the following questions as you watch and listen to the teaching.

Background

1. Who wrote the book of Samuel, and why is this important to understand?

_____

_____

2. What were the main events that 1 Samuel covered?

_____

_____

_____

3. What is a major theme related to God in 1 and 2 Samuel? How is that theme portrayed in the recorded events of David's life?

_____

_____

_____

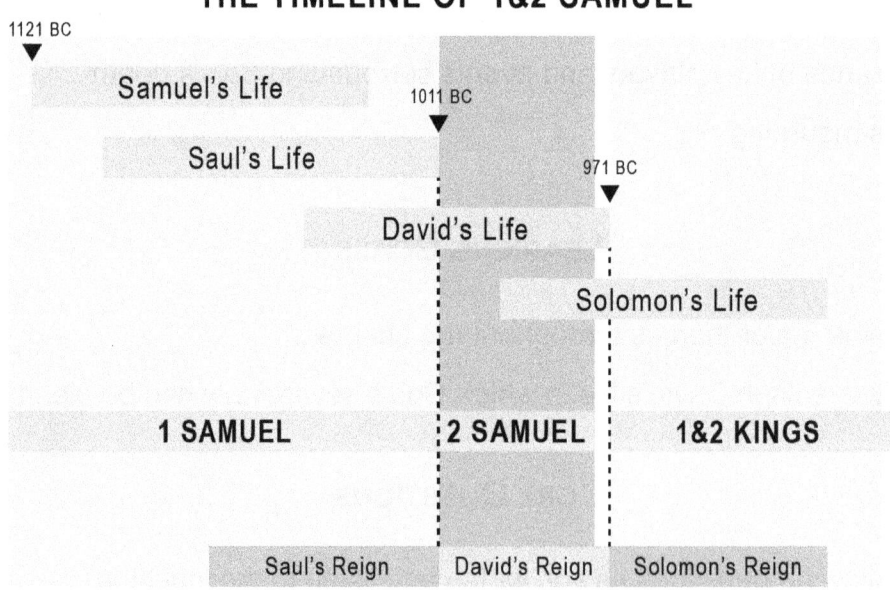

THE TIMELINE OF 1 & 2 SAMUEL

David Mourns Saul's Death: Chapter 1

2 Samuel 1:1

4. Where in Judah did David and his men remain for two days after defeating the Amalekites? What was the significance of this location?

_____

_____

_____

2 Samuel 1:2

5. What is the significance of it being the third day when the messenger arrived at David's camp?

_____

_____

_____

2 Samuel 1:3–4

6. Which two main characters did the messenger inform David were dead? Why was this important for David's future kingship?

_____

_____

_____

2 Samuel 1:5–7

7. Where was Saul when the messenger found him, and what was he doing? Why wasn't he successful?

_____

_____

_____

2 Samuel 1:8–10

8. What did the messenger do when Saul asked him to kill him, and what reason did the messenger give to David for doing so?

___

___

___

2 Samuel 1:11–12

9. What did David and his men do when the messenger relayed the news?

___

___

___

2 Samuel 1:13

10. Where was the messenger from, and why did it matter to David? What emboldened the servant to reveal his true ethnicity?

___

___

___

2 Samuel 1:14–16

11. What three things did David do when the messenger answered his question?

___

___

___

David Mourns Saul's Death: Chapter 1

2 Samuel 1:17–18

12. How did David first mourn over Saul and Jonathan's deaths? What were the implications of their deaths?

_____
_____
_____

2 Samuel 1:19

13. What did David say to show his respect for Saul in this verse? Why did he choose those particular words?

_____
_____
_____

2 Samuel 1:20

14. Why did David not want the news of Saul's death to spread?

_____
_____
_____

2 Samuel 1:21

15. What did David pronounce over Gilboa, and why?

_____
_____
_____

2 Samuel 1:22–23

16. What praises did David proclaim over Saul and Jonathan?

_____

_____

_____

2 Samuel 1:24

17. Why did David tell the daughters of Israel to lament Saul's passing? Why would this have been significant to the nation?

_____

_____

_____

2 Samuel 1:25–27

18. At the end of the lament, over whom did David mourn the most, and what long-term effects might this person's death have had on David's future decisions as king?

_____

_____

_____

DISCUSSION QUESTIONS

1. A major theme in 1 and 2 Samuel is God's sovereignty. In what ways do we see God's sovereignty displayed in David's life?

_____

_____

_____

2. What is historically significant about the messenger's place of origin?

_____

_____

_____

3. Even though he had multiple chances, why did David never attack Saul?

_____

_____

_____

4. Do you think the messenger was telling the truth about being the one who killed Saul? Why or why not?

_____

_____

_____

DIGGING DEEPER (OPTIONAL)

Should you choose to dig deeper, complete the following Digging Deeper section.

In the lined note-taking spaces provided below, record what you observe in each passage and the questions you have about it.

Things to look for:

- Who is speaking?
- To whom is he speaking?
- What does this passage say about God, about Jesus, about the church, and about individual believers?
- What do readers of this text stand to gain?

2 Samuel

Scripture Passages:

1 Samuel 14:6–15

Romans 13:1–7

1 Timothy 2:1–4

1 Samuel 13:8–14

1 Samuel 15:17–31

Acts 13:21–22

Deuteronomy 17:14–17

OBSERVATIONS

_____
_____
_____
_____
_____
_____
_____
_____
_____
_____
_____
_____
_____
_____

DAVID MOURNS SAUL'S DEATH: CHAPTER 1

QUESTIONS

A LITTLE DEEPER...

1. What does 1 Samuel 13:14 mean by "a man after His own heart," and to whom does this verse refer? In what ways did this description not apply to Saul?

2. How do Romans 13:1–7 and 1 Timothy 2:1–4 change the way you view governing authorities and your understanding of God's will for your behavior toward them?

3. David's taking of multiple wives was evidence of a sinful pattern in his life. According to Deuteronomy 17:17, what is one reason this was unlawful for David to do?

_____

_____

_____

SESSION 2

Divided Kingdom, Divided Heart: Chapters 2:1–32 & 3:1–16

Read 2 Samuel 2:1–32 & 3:1–16.

TOPIC OVERVIEW

- A divided kingdom
- Changing alliances

LEARNING GOALS

- Identify key characters in the Israel vs. Judah conflict.
- Gain a better understanding of David's heart for God vs. his weakness for women.

CORE QUESTIONS

Answer the following questions as you watch and listen to the teaching.

2 SAMUEL

2 Samuel 2:1

1. When David asked the Lord if he should go to Judah, what was God's response, and where did He tell David to go? What was the significance of this location in particular?

_____
_____
_____

2 Samuel 2:2–3

2. Whom did David take with him?

_____
_____
_____

2 Samuel 2:4

3. What did the men of Judah do when David and his people settled into the cities?

_____
_____
_____

2 Samuel 2:5–7

4. How did David respond when he heard who buried Saul? Why was this important to David?

_____
_____
_____

2 Samuel 2:8

5. Who was Abner, and what did he do in response to David being anointed king?

_____

_____

_____

2 Samuel 2:9

6. What significant events took place in response to Abner's action?

_____

_____

_____

2 Samuel 2:10

7. Whom did the house of Judah follow? How was the nation divided politically?

_____

_____

_____

2 Samuel 2:11

8. How long did David reign over the house of Judah? How long was Ish-bosheth's reign?

_____

_____

_____

2 Samuel 2:12–13

9. Who met at the pool of Gibeon, and what were their allegiances?

_____

_____

_____

2 Samuel 2:14–15

10. What was the proposal for this attempted peace treaty? Why would they have proposed such a battle?

_____

_____

_____

2 Samuel 2:16–17

11. What was the result of the battle?

_____

_____

_____

2 Samuel 2:18

12. Who were the three brothers present at the battle?

_____

_____

_____

2 Samuel 2:19–20

13. Who pursued Abner, and what was his greatest skill?

_____

_____

_____

2 Samuel 2:21–22

14. What did Abner try to convince Asahel to do, and why?

_____

_____

_____

2 Samuel 2:23

15. What was Asahel's fate?

_____

_____

_____

16. What were the possible reasons for Abner using the butt end of his spear?

_____

_____

_____

2 Samuel 2:24–25

17. Where did Joab and Abishai finally catch up with Abner?

_____

_____

_____

2 SAMUEL

18. Who rallied behind Abner? Why did they side with him?

___

2 Samuel 2:26–27

19. Who was ultimately to blame for the battle?

___

2 Samuel 2:28

20. Why did Joab blow the trumpet to stop the pursuit of Israel?

___

2 Samuel 2:29

21. Where did Abner and his men return after the battle? What made this location significant?

___

2 Samuel 2:30–31

22. How many men from each side were killed?

2 Samuel 2:32

23. Where did Joab bury Asahel?

2 Samuel 3:1

24. What was the long-term result of Abner's ill-advised combat? What was the ultimate outcome of the long war between the houses of Saul and David?

2 Samuel 3:2–5

25. Who were the children born to David at Hebron?

26. Although unlawful by God's command, David had many wives. What is the most likely reason most of the marriages were made?

_____
_____
_____

2 Samuel 3:6–7

27. How was Abner making himself strong in the house of Saul? Why was this considered a power play?

_____
_____
_____

28. How was this a betrayal of Ish-bosheth?

_____
_____
_____

2 Samuel 3:8

29. How did Abner defend himself against the king's accusations? Why did he present himself as insulted instead of denying the charges?

_____
_____
_____

Divided Kingdom, Divided Heart: Chapters 5:1–32 & 3:1–16

2 Samuel 3:9–11

30. What was Abner's threat to Ish-bosheth, and how did Ish-bosheth respond?

___

2 Samuel 3:12

31. What did Abner tell David he would do?

___

2 Samuel 3:13

32. What was David's condition for making the treaty?

___

2 Samuel 3:14–15

33. What price did David have to pay before Saul gave him Michal as a wife?

___

34. Who was Michal with when Ish-bosheth took her?

___

2 Samuel 3:16

35. What was significant about the husband's response to Michal being taken from him? How did this reflect on David's character at that time?

___

DISCUSSION QUESTIONS

1. In Deuteronomy 17, the Lord strictly commanded that the king should not take multiple wives for himself. Other than political strategy, what could be a reason David continuously broke this law?

___

2. In 2 Samuel 3, we see David's family line grow as he waited to become king over all of Israel. What are some ways the Lord made connections between David (during this time) and Jesus?

___

3. What were David's real intentions in asking for Michal to be returned to him?

___

DIGGING DEEPER (OPTIONAL)

Should you choose to dig deeper, complete the following Digging Deeper section.

In the lined note-taking spaces provided below, record what you observe in each passage and the questions you have about it.

Things to look for:

- Who is speaking?
- To whom is he speaking?
- What does this passage say about God, about Jesus, about the church, and about individual believers?
- What do readers of this text stand to gain?

Scripture Passages:

1 John 5:14–15

Deuteronomy 7:1–6

Deuteronomy 24:1–4

Romans 12:17–21

Matthew 18:21–35

OBSERVATIONS

_____
_____
_____
_____
_____
_____
_____
_____
_____

QUESTIONS

A LITTLE DEEPER…

1. David sought the will of God by asking Him specific questions, and David received specific answers. How often do you take advantage of the opportunity to seek God's counsel in prayer when trying to make a decision? Do you wait for and listen to the response? In what form(s) does it come?

2. In what ways did David disobey God in matters of marriage? Why was it wrong for David to take Michal back as his wife?

_____

_____

_____

3. How does God instruct believers to behave toward people who wrong them? What are His views on revenge?

_____

_____

_____

2 Samuel

SESSIONS 3–4

David's Obstacles Fall: Chapters 3:17–39; 4; & 5:1–5

Read 2 Samuel 3:17–39; 4; & 5:1–5.

TOPIC OVERVIEW

- Abner's death
- David's response to lawbreakers

LEARNING GOALS

- Identify points in the chapters where God used crimes of passion to bring about His will.
- Observe David's faith in God's plan for his kingship.

CORE QUESTIONS

Answer the following questions as you watch and listen to the teaching.

Background

1. What did Abner do in response to Ish-bosheth confronting him?

_____

_____

_____

2. What did David do in response to Abner's proposal for a covenant between them?

_____

_____

_____

2 Samuel 3:17–18

3. Whom did Abner consult with, and what did he tell them?

_____

_____

_____

2 Samuel 3:19

4. Who else did Abner speak with to rally the people for David? How was this ironic, given Abner's history with the people?

_____

_____

_____

2 Samuel 3:20

5. What did David do for Abner after his political campaigning? Why was this significant?

_____

_____

_____

2 Samuel 3:21

6. Before David sent Abner away in peace, what did Abner request from him?

_____

_____

_____

2 Samuel 3:22

7. Where was Joab while this was going on? Whom had he been fighting?

_____

_____

_____

2 Samuel 3:23–25

8. What did Joab tell David that Abner came to do?

_____

_____

_____

9. Why was Joab so upset?

_____

_____

_____

2 Samuel 3:26–27

10. In his anger, what did Joab do after leaving David?

_____

_____

_____

2 Samuel 3:28

11. What was David's first declaration after hearing of Abner's death?

_____
_____
_____

2 Samuel 3:29

12. Why was David's response to Joab's crime unusual?

_____
_____
_____

2 Samuel 3:30

13. Who else was involved in the conspiracy to kill Abner?

_____
_____
_____

2 Samuel 3:31

14. How did David show respect to Abner and declare innocence in his death?

_____
_____
_____

2 Samuel 3:32–34

15. During the funeral procession and burial, what were the main points David made in his lament?

_____
_____
_____

2 Samuel 3:35

16. Why did David refuse to eat?

_____
_____
_____

2 Samuel 3:36–37

17. What was the people's response to David's mourning?

_____
_____
_____

2 Samuel 3:38–39

18. As David continued to mourn and honor Abner, what did he say about the Lord? How does this reflect on David as a leader?

_____
_____
_____

2 Samuel 4:1

19. What are three reasons Ish-bosheth lost courage after hearing of Abner's death?

_____

_____

_____

2 Samuel 4:2–3

20. Who were the two military commanders from the tribe of Benjamin? What was significant about the town they were from?

_____

_____

_____

2 Samuel 4:4

21. Other than Ish-bosheth, who was the only other living relative of Saul? What made him unique?

_____

_____

_____

2 Samuel 4:5–6

22. What was Rechab and Baanah's crime against Ish-bosheth?

_____

_____

_____

2 Samuel 4:7

23. What did Rechab and Baanah do after killing Ish-bosheth?

_____
_____
_____

2 Samuel 4:8

24. Why did the men present the head of Ish-bosheth to David?

_____
_____
_____

2 Samuel 4:9–11

25. What was David's response to their presentation?

_____
_____
_____

2 Samuel 4:12

26. How were the men killed?

_____
_____
_____

27. What did David and his men do with the head of Ish-bosheth?

_____
_____
_____

2 SAMUEL

DISCUSSION QUESTIONS

1. David put Joab's punishment into God's hands. What are three reasons it is better to "leave room for the wrath of God," as Paul said (Romans 12:19)?

_____

_____

_____

2. After learning of Ish-bosheth's death, David punished the men who intended to avenge him. What was David declaring by doing this?

_____

_____

_____

3. What is the historical significance of David hanging the two men's bodies by the pool in Hebron?

_____

_____

_____

DIGGING DEEPER (OPTIONAL)

Should you choose to dig deeper, complete the following Digging Deeper section.

In the lined note-taking spaces provided below, record what you observe in each passage and the questions you have about it.

Things to look for:

- Who is speaking?
- To whom is he speaking?
- What does this passage say about God, about Jesus, about the church, and about individual believers?
- What do readers of this text stand to gain?

Scripture Passages:

Psalm 6

Proverbs 3:5–6

Romans 8:31

Isaiah 55:8–9

1 Chronicles 11:4–7

1 Samuel 4:1–11

OBSERVATIONS

_____
_____
_____
_____
_____
_____
_____
_____
_____
_____
_____
_____

QUESTIONS

_____
_____
_____

A Little Deeper…

1. How and why did David's actions and responses often defy other people's expectations?

2. According to 1 Chronicles 11, how did Joab distinguish himself in the attack on the city of Jebus?

3. How did the ark of the Lord end up in the hands of the Philistines?

SESSIONS 5–6

Walking in the Will of God: Chapter 5 & 6:1–5

Read 2 Samuel 5 & 6:1–5.

TOPIC OVERVIEW

- David's establishment of Jerusalem as the city of David
- David's political and religious successes

LEARNING GOALS

- What were David's pre-battle habits that ensured his success?
- Why did God still hold David accountable when he disobeyed but had pure motives?

CORE QUESTIONS

Answer the following questions as you watch and listen to the teaching.

2 Samuel 5:6

1. What did the people of Jebus tell David when David and his men arrived? What gave David the confidence to ignore their claims?

_____

_____

_____

2 Samuel 5:7–8

2. What was David's response to their threat?

_____

_____

_____

2 Samuel 5:9–10

3. David set up his kingdom and called it the "City of David." What was the key factor in David's success?

_____

_____

_____

2 Samuel 5:11

4. Who built a house for David? What did he provide?

_____

_____

_____

2 Samuel 5:12

5. According to this verse, for whose sake did the Lord establish David as king over Israel?

_____

_____

_____

2 Samuel 5:13

6. Even though God established David as king, he still entertained what unlawful practice?

_____

_____

_____

2 Samuel 5:14–16

7. What were the names of the children born to David in Jerusalem?

_____

_____

_____

2 Samuel 5:17

8. Who rose against David after he was anointed king? Why did they attack so quickly?

_____

_____

_____

2 Samuel 5:18–19

9. What was the first thing David did when faced with the enemy?

_____
_____
_____

10. What was God's reply to David, and what did He provide?

_____
_____
_____

2 Samuel 5:20

11. Where did David defeat the Philistines? What was the significance of the name David gave to the location?

_____
_____
_____

12. Whom did David credit for the victory against the Philistines?

_____
_____
_____

2 Samuel 5:21

13. What did the Philistines abandon, and what happened to them?

_____
_____
_____

2 Samuel 5:22

14. Where did the Philistines set up camp? What was significant about this location, based on its name?

_____

_____

_____

2 Samuel 5:23–24

15. When David inquired of the Lord whether he should attack, what were the Lord's instructions?

_____

_____

_____

2 Samuel 5:25

16. What was the result of the battle?

_____

_____

_____

2 Samuel 6:1–2

17. Why did David gather thirty thousand chosen men of Israel? What was significant about the name of the location?

_____

_____

_____

2 Samuel 6:3

18. What was wrong with the way David transported the ark?

_____
_____
_____

19. From whose house was the ark of the Lord retrieved?

_____
_____
_____

2 Samuel 6:5

20. David's motives were pure, although his obedience was not. In what manner did David transport the ark of the Lord?

_____
_____
_____

DISCUSSION QUESTIONS

1. Which mountains and valleys surrounded Jerusalem?

_____
_____
_____

2. How did this landscape protect the city?

_____
_____
_____

WALKING IN THE WILL OF GOD: CHAPTER 5 & 6:5

3. What did the term "blind and lame" become a euphemism for in Israel?

_____

_____

_____

4. Whom was David comparable to, regarding his large family of multiple wives and his children by them?

_____

_____

_____

5. Who are the two children of David mentioned in Jesus' genealogy, and what makes them significant?

_____

_____

_____

6. How did Saul go against God's wishes regarding the ark of the Lord?

_____

_____

_____

DIGGING DEEPER (OPTIONAL)

Should you choose to dig deeper, complete the following Digging Deeper section.

In the lined note-taking spaces provided below, record what you observe in each passage and the questions you have about it.

2 Samuel

Things to look for:

- Who is speaking?
- To whom is he speaking?
- What does this passage say about God, about Jesus, about the church, and about individual believers?
- What do readers of this text stand to gain?

Scripture Passages:

Matthew 17:20

Matthew 19:26

James 1:2–8

Luke 11:27–28

Hebrews 4:12

2 Timothy 3:14–17

Numbers 4:1–20

OBSERVATIONS

_____

_____

_____

_____

_____

_____

_____

Questions

A Little Deeper...

1. What does it mean for believers to act in faith? How did David exercise faith in God before becoming king over all of Israel? How did he show faith in his approach to military strategy?

2. What value does Bible study hold for believers today? How often do you turn to God's word when you are wondering what to do in a particular situation?

_____

_____

_____

3. What was the proper way to transport the ark of the Lord? What consequence did God lay out for unlawful handling of the holy objects?

_____

_____

_____

SESSION 7A

True Worship Is Obedience: Chapters 6:6–23 & 7:1–16

Read 2 Samuel 6:6–23 & 7:1–16.

TOPIC OVERVIEW

- The lesson of Uzzah
- David's shift in obedience to God
- Michal's bitterness toward David

LEARNING GOALS

- Understand the importance of obedience to God, not just relying on pure motives.
- Identify points of humility in David's mistakes and worship.

Core Questions

Background

2 Samuel 6:1–5

1. From where did David and his men retrieve the ark of the Lord?

2. How did the Lord instruct the people to move the ark of the Lord?

3. Whom did David gather to go with him to retrieve the ark of the Lord, and how many were there?

4. Who was leading the new cart carrying the ark of the Lord?

Answer the following questions as you watch and listen to the teaching.

2 Samuel 6:6

5. What did Uzzah do to the ark of the Lord?

_____

_____

_____

2 Samuel 6:7

6. Why was God angry with Uzzah?

_____

_____

_____

7. How was Uzzah being irreverent by trying to protect the ark?

_____

_____

_____

2 Samuel 6:8–9

8. David became angry with the Lord for striking Uzzah as a punishment. What emotion did David have, along with anger, that affected his next decision?

_____

_____

_____

2 Samuel 6:10–11

9. What did David decide to do after the Lord's punishment, and what was the result of David refusing to bring the ark into Jerusalem?

___

___

___

2 Samuel 6:12

10. What changed David's mind about reinstating the plan to bring the ark into Jerusalem?

___

___

___

2 Samuel 6:13

11. What did David do in repentance as they brought the ark back to the tabernacle?

___

___

___

2 Samuel 6:14–15

12. How were David and the people celebrating on the way back to Jerusalem?

___

___

___

13. What was David wearing, and why?

2 Samuel 6:16

14. Why did Michal despise David when she saw him return with the ark?

2 Samuel 6:17–18

15. What was the first thing David did after bringing the ark into the prepared tent?

2 Samuel 6:19

16. Which gifts from his storehouse did David give to the people?

17. What did the gifts represent?

2 Samuel 6:20

18. What was Michal's primary complaint to David?

2 Samuel 6:21–22

19. How did David correct his wife, and whom did he credit for his kingship?

20. What character trait did David show in his response to her?

2 Samuel 6:21–23

21. What was significant about the fact that Michal never had a child?

2 Samuel 7:1–3

22. David had rest from all his enemies, but he was bothered that the ark of God was in a meager tent. What did the prophet Nathan tell him?

___

2 Samuel 7:4–7

23. What did the Lord tell Nathan the prophet in response to his initial words to David?

___

2 Samuel 7:8

24. How did God gently remind David of his place?

___

2 Samuel 7:9–11

25. What did the Lord promise David?

___

2 Samuel 7:12–13

26. What did the Lord tell David would happen after he died?

_____

_____

_____

2 Samuel 7:14–16

27. What did God promise would happen when his son would inevitably fall into sin?

_____

_____

_____

28. What is this set of promises the Lord made to David called?

_____

_____

_____

Discussion Questions

1. If God had not acted against Uzzah, then He would have been violating His word in Numbers 4. What would have happened if God had made an exception for Uzzah and not kept His word?

_____

_____

_____

2. David became angry and fearful of God when He killed Uzzah. Why do we often feel that way toward God when we endure His discipline?

_____

_____

_____

3. Why does the Bible place such high demands of character and knowledge on anyone who would lead God's people?

_____

_____

_____

4. David immediately recognized that Michal's true concerns were not with his dignity as king. What was her outburst about?

_____

_____

_____

DIGGING DEEPER (OPTIONAL)

Should you choose to dig deeper, complete the following Digging Deeper section.

In the lined note-taking spaces provided below, record what you observe in each passage and the questions you have about it.

Things to look for:

- Who is speaking?
- To whom is he speaking?
- What does this passage say about God, about Jesus, about the church, and about individual believers?
- What do readers of this text stand to gain?

2 Samuel

Scripture Passages:

Numbers 23:19

Psalm 33:1–12

Isaiah 40:8

Psalm 119

Luke 11:27–28

1 John 2:3

Hebrews 12:28

1 Chronicles 15

Luke 1:30–33

OBSERVATIONS

_____
_____
_____
_____
_____
_____
_____
_____
_____
_____
_____
_____

TRUE WORSHIP IS OBEDIENCE: CHAPTERS 6:6–23 & 7:1–16

QUESTIONS

_____
_____
_____
_____
_____
_____
_____
_____
_____
_____
_____
_____
_____
_____

A LITTLE DEEPER…

1. Why are the unchanging nature of God and the reliability of His word important? What responsibility do believers have regarding the word of God?

_____
_____
_____

2. How and why was David careful to obey God in his second attempt to transport the ark of the Lord to Jerusalem? How did David serve as a picture of Christ on that day?

_____
_____
_____

2 SAMUEL

3. Who is the ultimate fulfillment of the Davidic Covenant, according to Luke 1?

_____

_____

_____

SESSION 7B

Awaiting a Promised Kingdom: Chapter 7

Read 2 Samuel 7.

TOPIC OVERVIEW

- God's revelation to David
- Fulfillment of the Abrahamic and Davidic Covenants through Christ

LEARNING GOALS

- Observe David's heart of humility in receiving the Lord's revelation.
- Identify the fulfillment of God's covenants through the future coming of Jesus.

CORE QUESTIONS

Background

2 Samuel 7:4–16

1. What was the likely reason David proposed to build God a temple in place of the tent?

_____
_____
_____

2. To interpret the covenants of God, including the Davidic Covenant, properly, the law of suggested fulfillment can be used. How does this explain the delayed fulfillment?

_____

_____

_____

3. In the Abrahamic and Davidic Covenants, who is the future King that God was referencing, and which kingdom will He bring?

_____

_____

_____

4. Which new details did the Lord give in the Davidic Covenant that were never given to Abraham?

_____

_____

_____

Answer the following questions as you watch and listen to the teaching.

2 Samuel 7:17–18

5. What was the first thing David did when the prophet Nathan told him not to build a house for God?

_____

_____

_____

2 Samuel 7:19–21

6. What was David in awe of as he was praying?

_____

_____

_____

2 Samuel 7:22–24

7. For whom did God redeem Israel, and why?

_____

_____

_____

2 Samuel 7:25

8. What did David pray the Lord would do after he received this word from Him?

_____

_____

_____

2 Samuel 7:26–27

9. What gave David the courage to pray?

_____

_____

_____

2 SAMUEL

2 Samuel 7:28–29

10. What did David request of God?

_____
_____
_____

DISCUSSION QUESTIONS

1. In verse 7, the Lord reminded David that God never commanded Israel to build His house in any form other than a tent. What is good advice to follow when deciding whether to take on another task for the Lord?

_____
_____
_____

2. What were the three errors David made in assuming he could build God a house for the ark of the Lord?

_____
_____
_____

3. In what two ways did the fulfillment of prophetic events from the days of Joshua up to David not fulfill the Abrahamic Covenant?

_____
_____
_____

4. When Jesus returns, how long does Revelation 20 say His kingdom will last?

_____
_____
_____

AWAITING A PROMISED KINGDOM: CHAPTER 7

5. What are two ways we know that David's son Solomon was not the fulfillment of the coming king the Lord referenced in His revelation?

_____

_____

_____

DIGGING DEEPER (OPTIONAL)

Should you choose to dig deeper, complete the following Digging Deeper section.

In the lined note-taking spaces provided below, record what you observe in each passage and the questions you have about it.

Things to look for:

- Who is speaking?
- To whom is he speaking?
- What does this passage say about God, about Jesus, about the church, and about individual believers?
- What do readers of this text stand to gain?

Scripture Passages:

Genesis 49:10

Isaiah 2:1–4

Isaiah 9:2–7

Isaiah 11

Revelation 3:21

Genesis 26:3–4

Deuteronomy 30:4–7

2 Samuel

Hebrews 11

2 Peter 3

1 Samuel 18:1–4

1 Samuel 20:12–17

Observations

Questions

A Little Deeper...

1. How does Scripture describe the coming kingdom of the Messiah?

2. How can believers today demonstrate faith as they await the fulfillment of God's promises?

3. What covenant did Jonathan and David make with each other?

though # 2 Samuel

SESSIONS 8–9

A God Who Keeps Lovingkindness: Chapters 8 & 9

Read 2 Samuel 8 & 9.

TOPIC OVERVIEW

- Military successes of King David
- David's merciful faithfulness in keeping his covenant with Jonathan

LEARNING GOALS

- Review the military victories that God helped David achieve.
- Draw connections between David's mercy toward Mephibosheth and Jesus' mercy toward us.

CORE QUESTIONS

Background

1. What blessings did David experience as a result of God's anointing?

_____

_____

_____

2 SAMUEL

2. What did the Lord promise David through His covenant with him?

_____

_____

_____

Answer the following questions as you watch and listen to the teaching.

2 Samuel 8:1

3. What was significant about the city that David overthrew?

_____

_____

_____

2 Samuel 8:2

4. How did David divide the defeated Moabites, and for what purpose?

_____

_____

_____

2 Samuel 8:3–4

5. When David defeated Hadadezer—the son of Rehob, king of Zobah—what did he do with the chariot horses he captured? Why would he do this?

_____

_____

_____

2 Samuel 8:5–6

6. What did David do with the Arameans when they arrived to help Hadadezer?

_____

_____

_____

2 Samuel 8:7–10

7. What precious metals did David take back to Jerusalem from his conquests?

_____

_____

_____

2 Samuel 8:11–12

8. What did David do with the precious spoils of the nations he subdued?

_____

_____

_____

2 Samuel 8:13–14

9. David's military victories brought extensive wealth to Israel and boosted his reputation. To what did the writer attribute David's victories?

_____

_____

_____

2 Samuel 8:15

10. What was David known for during his reign over Israel?

2 Samuel 8:16–18

11. What position did Joab hold in David's kingdom? What positions did David's sons hold?

2 Samuel 9:1

12. Why did David want to show kindness to a living family member of Saul?

2 Samuel 9:2–3

13. Who did Ziba, the servant of the house, tell David was still living?

2 Samuel 9:4–5

14. What did David do when he heard of Jonathan's son?

_____

_____

_____

2 Samuel 9:6

15. What was Mephibosheth's reaction to being summoned to David?

_____

_____

_____

2 Samuel 9:7

16. What three things did David tell Mephibosheth he would do for him?

_____

_____

_____

2 Samuel 9:8

17. Why did Mephibosheth call himself a dead dog?

_____

_____

_____

2 Samuel

2 Samuel 9:9–10

18. What command did David give to the servant Ziba? What are the likely reasons David assigned this lesser post to him?

_____

_____

_____

2 Samuel 9:11

19. Who else ate with the king at his table?

_____

_____

_____

Discussion Questions

1. Why did David have the men of Moab lie on the ground?

_____

_____

_____

2. What was the significance of David having many defeated enemies become servants instead of wiping them out?

_____

_____

_____

3. What were the details of David's covenant with Jonathan?

_____

_____

_____

4. What was the significance of Mephibosheth being invited to eat regularly at the king's table?

_____

_____

_____

DIGGING DEEPER (OPTIONAL)

Should you choose to dig deeper, complete the following Digging Deeper section.

In the lined note-taking spaces provided below, record what you observe in each passage and the questions you have about it.

Things to look for:

- Who is speaking?
- To whom is he speaking?
- What does this passage say about God, about Jesus, about the church, and about individual believers?
- What do readers of this text stand to gain?

Scripture Passages:

Exodus 34:5–7

Exodus 20:5–6

Psalm 23

Psalm 25:4–7

Matthew 15:21–28

Revelation 3:20

2 Samuel

Ephesians 2:4–10

James 1:12–27

Observations

Questions

A LITTLE DEEPER…

1. In what ways has God extended lovingkindness to you? How have you received and responded to it?

2. In what ways can you extend lovingkindness to the people in your life, including those who have wronged you?

3. How does temptation work? How does it take hold and lead to sin? What is the end result?

2 Samuel

SESSIONS 10–11

A Corrupted Heart: Chapters 10 & 11

Read 2 Samuel 10 & 11.

TOPIC OVERVIEW

- David's neglect of leadership duties
- David's fall into sin

LEARNING GOALS

- Understand the sequence of events that lead a person to sin.
- Reflect on the heart change that occurs when God is not sought first.

CORE QUESTIONS

Background

1. In chapter 9, we see Mephibosheth crippled and on his face before King David. How is this an image of us as human beings?

_____

_____

_____

2. How did David's response to Mephibosheth present a picture of Jesus?

3. What did David give Mephibosheth that would set the stage for future conflict?

Answer the following questions as you watch and listen to the teaching.

2 Samuel 10:1–2

4. What did David do for the new king of the Ammonites when his father died?

2 Samuel 10:3

5. What did the Ammonite princes tell the king that David was actually doing?

2 Samuel 10:4

6. What did King Hanun do to David's servants?

A CORRUPTED HEART: CHAPTERS 10 & 11

7. What made these actions so insulting to David's men?

_____
_____
_____

2 Samuel 10:5

8. How did David sensitively reassure his men when they were humiliated?

_____
_____
_____

2 Samuel 10:6

9. What were the Ammonites expecting when they hired military help from their allies?

_____
_____
_____

2 Samuel 10:7–8

10. When David heard that the Ammonites and Arameans were gathering for war, he sent Joab and his army to the front. What was different about this response versus the other battles David had fought?

_____
_____
_____

2 Samuel 10:9–11

11. Joab divided the troops and set his brother, Abishai, over the second half. Who were the two enemy groups they were set against? Why did he assign the second troop to his brother?

_____
_____
_____

2 Samuel 10:12

12. What was Joab's rally cry to his fighting men?

_____
_____
_____

2 Samuel 10:13–14

13. What was the outcome of the battle?

_____
_____
_____

14. Joab returned to Jerusalem without pursuing the fleeing enemy. What did this mean for the future?

_____
_____
_____

A Corrupted Heart: Chapters 10 & 11

2 Samuel 10:15–16

15. What did King Hadadezer of Zobah do to strengthen his rivalry with David?

_____
_____
_____

2 Samuel 10:17–18

16. David went to war with the Arameans and was victorious. Which significant character did he kill in the battle?

_____
_____
_____

2 Samuel 10:19

17. What did the servants of Hadadezer do after David defeated them?

_____
_____
_____

2 Samuel 11:1

18. What did David do in the spring that would have been considered wrong for kings to do?

_____
_____
_____

19. What did this action suggest about David's leadership at this point?

2 Samuel 11:2

20. What was the likely reason David was walking on his rooftop in the evening?

21. Based on the location of Bathsheba's home, what does her bathing on the rooftop at that time of day imply?

2 Samuel 11:3–4

22. What does James 1:14–15 say about the spiral into sin?

2 Samuel 11:5

23. What was the immediate result of their adultery? What did the law require for their sin, based on Leviticus 20:10?

A Corrupted Heart: Chapters 10 & 11

2 Samuel 11:6–7

24. Rather than confessing and seeking Uriah's forgiveness, what did David inquire about when he summoned Uriah from the battlefront?

_____

_____

_____

2 Samuel 11:8–9

25. In what way did Uriah honorably disobey the king?

_____

_____

_____

26. What was David's purpose behind this, and how did Uriah's actions frustrate his plans?

_____

_____

_____

2 Samuel 11:10–11

27. When David asked him why he refused to go to his home, what was Uriah's response?

_____

_____

_____

2 Samuel 11:12

28. What was David's next command to Uriah?

_____

_____

_____

2 Samuel 11:13

29. After the first attempt failed, what was David's second attempt to have Uriah sleep with his wife?

_____

_____

_____

2 Samuel 11:14–15

30. What was David's command to Joab as his final attempt to hide his adultery?

_____

_____

_____

2 Samuel 11:16–17

31. David's command was obeyed, and all went according to plan. However, who else suffered from this decision?

_____

_____

_____

A Corrupted Heart: Chapters 10 & 11

2 Samuel 11:18–21

32. What was the purpose of delaying the news of Uriah's death until after David was upset about the battle plan that was executed?

___

___

___

2 Samuel 11:22–25

33. What was David's response to Joab regarding Uriah's death?

___

___

___

2 Samuel 11:26–27

34. When Bathsheba's mourning period for her husband was over, what did David do?

___

___

___

35. What was the divine judgment on David's actions?

___

___

___

DISCUSSION QUESTIONS

1. What could David have done when he first saw Bathsheba bathing instead of allowing his lust to lead him to adultery and murder?

___

___

___

2. What was interesting about Bathsheba bathing *after* she and David engaged in adultery?

___

___

___

3. Based on Genesis 3:6, what is a person's instinctive response after engaging in sin?

___

___

___

DIGGING DEEPER (OPTIONAL)

Should you choose to dig deeper, complete the following Digging Deeper section.

In the lined note-taking spaces provided below, record what you observe in each passage and the questions you have about it.

Things to look for:

- Who is speaking?
- To whom is he speaking?
- What does this passage say about God, about Jesus, about the church, and about individual believers?
- What do readers of this text stand to gain?

A Corrupted Heart: Chapters 10 & 11

Scripture Passages:

1 Corinthians 12

Acts 6:1–4

1 John 2:1–6, 12, 15–17

Psalm 51

Observations

Questions

A Little Deeper...

1. If you know the purpose to which God is calling you, consider what it would look like to continue serving that purpose with the gift God has given you. On the other hand, what would it look like to step away from that responsibility, even if you were to continue doing good? Who might miss out and in what ways?

2. David delegated his leadership position, choosing to send the army of Israel into battle while he remained behind in Jerusalem, and he ended up following the path of temptation into sin. What is the value in being where you're supposed to be, doing what you're supposed to be doing? What is the danger in operating outside of God's will?

3. When we know we have sinned, what is the right way to respond? What should we do, and when should we do it? How do we keep sin from escalating uncontrollably?

SESSION 12

Sin Exposed: Chapter 12

Read 2 Samuel 12.

TOPIC OVERVIEW

- David's sin revealed
- Divine judgment over sin

LEARNING GOALS

- Observe David's humility in enduring the death of his son.
- Understand the Lord's process of refining and restoring His sinful children.

CORE QUESTIONS

Answer the following questions as you watch and listen to the teaching.

2 Samuel 12:1–4

1. Whom did God enlist to confront David about his sin?

_____

_____

_____

2 SAMUEL

2. Whom did the flocks and ewe lamb represent in Nathan's parable?

___

2 Samuel 12:5–6

3. What was David's natural response upon hearing of the rich man who took and killed the ewe lamb?

___

2 Samuel 12:7–8

4. When Nathan pronounced David guilty, what did he remind David that the Lord had done and would do?

___

2 Samuel 12:9–12

5. After revealing that David's sin was known, what four things did the Lord pronounce in judgment over the house of David?

___

SIN EXPOSED: CHAPTER 12

2 Samuel 12:13

6. What was David's first response to Nathan's pronouncement?

_____
_____
_____

7. Even after revealing everything, what amazing statement did Nathan make after David confessed?

_____
_____
_____

2 Samuel 12:14

8. Although he was forgiven, restitution still had to be made for David's murder of Uriah. What was the consequence of that sin? What did it cause among Israel's enemies?

_____
_____
_____

2 Samuel 12:15

9. What was the first punishment the Lord brought to pass?

_____
_____
_____

2 Samuel 12:16–17

10. What was David's response when his son became sick?

_____

_____

_____

2 Samuel 12:18–19

11. Why were David's servants whispering, and what were they afraid of when the boy died?

_____

_____

_____

2 Samuel 12:20

12. When David heard of his son's death, what was his first response?

_____

_____

_____

2 Samuel 12:21

13. Why were the servants confused by David's behavior?

_____

_____

_____

SIN EXPOSED: CHAPTER 12

2 Samuel 12:22–23

14. What was David's explanation for his behavior?

___
___
___

DISCUSSION QUESTIONS

1. How would events have played out differently if David had been devoted to his first and only wife, Michal?

___
___
___

2. God called David's sin despising the word of the Lord (2 Samuel 12:9). How did David sin against the word of the Lord?

___
___
___

3. In verse 10, Nathan said that the sword would never depart from David's house. What is the meaning of this euphemism? In what three specific ways would it come about?

___
___
___

4. About what did Nathan reassure David regarding David's sins?

___
___
___

2 SAMUEL

5. What are the four main reasons the Lord disciplines His children?

_____

_____

_____

DIGGING DEEPER (OPTIONAL)

Should you choose to dig deeper, complete the following Digging Deeper section.

In the lined note-taking spaces provided below, record what you observe in each passage and the questions you have about it.

Things to look for:

- Who is speaking?
- To whom is he speaking?
- What does this passage say about God, about Jesus, about the church, and about individual believers?
- What do readers of this text stand to gain?

Scripture Passages:

Psalm 38

1 John 1:5–10

Isaiah 55:7

Hebrews 4:14–16

Hebrews 12:4–11

Revelation 3:19

OBSERVATIONS

QUESTIONS

A LITTLE DEEPER...

1. What are the detrimental effects of unconfessed sin? Think of a time when you were confronted with your own sin. How did you respond, and what were the effects of that response? How might you respond differently if given another chance?

_____
_____
_____

2. What does Scripture encourage us to hope for and expect when we humbly confess our sins to God and repent?

_____
_____
_____

3. How does God's discipline differ from His wrath and His judgment? How should believers view God's discipline and respond to it? What are potential benefits of God's discipline?

_____
_____
_____

SESSION 13

The Consequences of David's Sin: Chapter 13:1–22

Read 2 Samuel 13:1–22.

TOPIC OVERVIEW

- The consequences of David's sin
- The birth of Solomon
- Amnon's sin

LEARNING GOALS

- Observe the unfolding of God's plan in the birth of Solomon.
- Understand the extent of God's grace as He reinstated David as a successful military leader.
- Identify the generational sin that came to fruition in Amnon's crimes.

2 SAMUEL

CORE QUESTIONS

Background

1. Why was it necessary for the Lord to expose and discipline David regarding his sin?

_____

_____

_____

2. According to Psalm 51:3–4, what did David recognize in the death of his son?

_____

_____

_____

3. After these events, David and Bathsheba conceived again. What two names were given to the boy, and why?

_____

_____

_____

4. What was God's promise in the Davidic Covenant?

_____

_____

_____

5. What do the terms *loved* and *hated* by God mean in reference to Solomon and Jacob?

_____

_____

_____

THE CONSEQUENCES OF DAVID'S SIN: CHAPTER 13:1–22

6. The Lord continued to bless David in warfare. Which people group did he defeat in 2 Samuel 12:26–31?

___

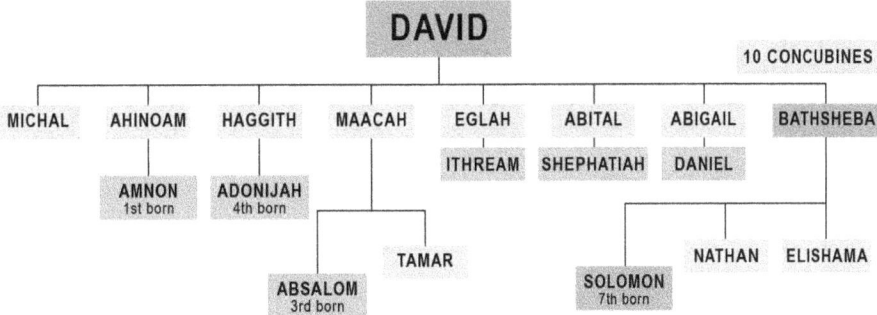

Answer the following questions as you watch and listen to the teaching.

2 Samuel 13:1–2

7. Who was Tamar, and who inappropriately longed for her?

___

2 Samuel 13:3

8. Who was the shrewd man who was friends with Amnon?

___

2 Samuel 13:4

9. What was Amnon's complaint to Jonadab?

_____

_____

_____

2 Samuel 13:5

10. What was Jonadab's advice to Amnon?

_____

_____

_____

11. Why did Jonadab want to help Amnon? How were his motives selfish?

_____

_____

_____

2 Samuel 13:6

12. Who was the first person Amnon manipulated when enacting Jonadab's plan?

_____

_____

_____

THE CONSEQUENCES OF DAVID'S SIN: CHAPTER 13:1–22

2 Samuel 13:7–8

13. Without hesitation, David ordered Tamar to prepare food for Amnon. Why did it matter if she made food in his sight?

_____
_____
_____

2 Samuel 13:9

14. What did Amnon refuse to do when Tamar prepared the food for him?

_____
_____
_____

2 Samuel 13:10–11

15. What did Amnon command Tamar to do?

_____
_____
_____

2 Samuel 13:12–13

16. What were Tamar's arguments against sleeping with her brother?

_____
_____
_____

2 Samuel 13:14

17. What was the result of Amnon's lust and Tamar's pleading?

___

2 Samuel 13:15

18. After the act, what did Amnon feel toward Tamar?

___

2 Samuel 13:16–17

19. Why would sending her away add to the evil of his action?

___

2 Samuel 13:18–19

20. What was Tamar's response to being thrown out of her brother's room?

___

2 Samuel 13:20

21. Why did Absalom tell Tamar to remain silent about the rape, and what kindness did Absalom show Tamar?

_____
_____
_____

Discussion Questions

1. Normally, the king's oldest son would be expected to inherit the throne, but Solomon was destined to rule after David. What was his placement in the succession?

_____
_____
_____

2. How did the birth of Solomon show God's blessing over His children, even when they sin?

_____
_____
_____

3. How did David's victory over the Ammonites sit as a bookend in the story of his sin?

_____
_____
_____

2 Samuel

4. How was what happened between Amnon and Tamar a consequence of David's sin of taking multiple wives?

_____

_____

_____

5. How would Jonadab's shrewdness help him in a battle between Amnon and Absalom?

_____

_____

_____

6. According to the law, what should have happened to Amnon after he raped Tamar?

_____

_____

_____

DIGGING DEEPER (OPTIONAL)

Should you choose to dig deeper, complete the following Digging Deeper section.

In the lined note-taking spaces provided below, record what you observe in each passage and the questions you have about it.

Things to look for:

- Who is speaking?
- To whom is he speaking?
- What does this passage say about God, about Jesus, about the church, and about individual believers?
- What do readers of this text stand to gain?

Scripture Passages:

Malachi 1:2–3

Romans 9:9–13

1 Chronicles 22:6–16

James 1:17–18

Ephesians 1:3–14

Ephesians 2:10

Ephesians 3:20–21

Galatians 6:7–9

OBSERVATIONS

QUESTIONS

A LITTLE DEEPER…

1. Why is it important to remember God's sovereignty? How is God's sovereignty comforting and encouraging? How can it be difficult to comprehend and accept?

2. How is consistent disobedience—whether in intentional rebellion, negligence, or carelessness—an attempt to mock God?

3. Have you ever mistaken God's mercy and grace for His approval? How can we avoid doing so?

_____

_____

_____

2 Samuel

SESSION 14

Systemic Issues in David's Family: Chapter 14

Read 2 Samuel 14.

TOPIC OVERVIEW

- Absalom's revenge
- David's refusal to administer justice
- The manipulation of David into pardoning Absalom

LEARNING GOALS

- Identify the sequence of events that led to further trouble in David's family.
- Examine the consequences of sin that is not handled appropriately.

CORE QUESTIONS

Background

1. Why would it have been natural for Absalom to invite the king and his family to shear the sheep in Baal-hazor?

_____

_____

_____

2 SAMUEL

2. In 2 Samuel 13:25–27, David turned down the invitation but agreed for Amnon and the other brothers to attend. Why would David have agreed, knowing the history of hatred between Absalom and Amnon?

___

3. How did Absalom plan to kill Amnon in 2 Samuel 13:28–29?

___

4. According to verses 30–31, what rumors spread to David before his sons had time to return to the palace?

___

5. What was Jonadab's part in the murder, and how was he able to reassure the king?

___

6. In 2 Samuel 13:34–36, we see David's sons returning home. How did Jonadab deliver this news to the king?

___

Systemic Issues in David's Family: Chapter 14

7. How long was Absalom in exile after killing his brother Amnon, and where did he go?

_____
_____
_____

Answer the following questions as you watch and listen to the teaching.

2 Samuel 14:1–3

8. What was Joab's purpose in having a woman pretend to be a mourner?

_____
_____
_____

2 Samuel 14:4–6

9. What lie did the woman tell David to set up a parallel story?

_____
_____
_____

2 Samuel 14:7

10. What was she asking for in light of her story?

_____
_____
_____

2 Samuel 14:8–10

11. What was David's response to the woman?

_____

_____

_____

2 Samuel 14:11

12. To get an immediate decision, she pressed David, saying that she feared for her and her son's lives due to the people who wanted justice. What did she convince David to do?

_____

_____

_____

2 Samuel 14:12–17

13. What was the primary argument the woman made for David to pardon Absalom?

_____

_____

_____

14. What biblical truth did the woman point out in an unbiblical fashion?

_____

_____

_____

SYSTEMIC ISSUES IN DAVID'S FAMILY: CHAPTER 14

2 Samuel 14:18–20

15. David suspected that the woman was lying, so he asked her if Joab was behind her story. What was her answer?

_____

_____

_____

2 Samuel 14:21

16. What did David tell Joab in response to the woman's story?

_____

_____

_____

2 Samuel 14:22–23

17. How did Joab react to the king? Whom did he retrieve after their conversation?

_____

_____

_____

2 Samuel 14:24

18. What was David's requirement upon Absalom's return?

_____

_____

_____

2 Samuel 14:25–27

19. What physical attributes was Absalom known for?

20. Who were Absalom's children?

2 Samuel 14:28

21. How long was Absalom in Jerusalem without seeing the king?

DISCUSSION QUESTIONS

1. How did Jonadab attempt a third angle with David at the news of Amnon's death?

2. In addition to God's discipline of taking the life of David's child, what were six other family consequences of David's poor choices up to this point?

SYSTEMIC ISSUES IN DAVID'S FAMILY: CHAPTER 14

3. According to Wiersbe, what are the results of grace?

_____

_____

_____

4. How did Amnon's murder solve a problem for David?

_____

_____

_____

DIGGING DEEPER (OPTIONAL)

Should you choose to dig deeper, complete the following Digging Deeper section.

In the lined note-taking spaces provided below, record what you observe in each passage and the questions you have about it.

Things to look for:

- Who is speaking?
- To whom is he speaking?
- What does this passage say about God, about Jesus, about the church, and about individual believers?
- What do readers of this text stand to gain?

Scripture Passages:

Romans 8:28–30

John 8:1–11

1 Samuel 16:6–7

Observations

Questions

A LITTLE DEEPER...

1. Think back to a sinful choice you made in the past. What were the consequences, or natural effects, of your sin over time? How far did they reach? How did God's mercy and grace show up along the way, even in those situations?

_____
_____
_____

2. What is the difference between mercy and license to sin? How did Jesus demonstrate both mercy and justice, each without neglecting or compromising the other?

_____
_____
_____

3. How does the way God sees human beings differ from the way we tend to see each other? How might it affect our choices if we were to try to view each other in a more godly way?

_____
_____
_____

2 Samuel

SESSION 15

David's Flight: Chapters 14:28–33 & 15

Read 2 Samuel 14:28–33 & 15.

TOPIC OVERVIEW

- Absalom's restoration to Jerusalem
- Absalom's political maneuvers
- David's exile into the wilderness

LEARNING GOALS

- Identify the direct consequences of David's refusal to judge according to God's laws.
- Evaluate David's heart changes as he fled Jerusalem.

CORE QUESTIONS

Answer the following questions as you watch and listen to the teaching.

2 Samuel 14:28

1. Why did Absalom live for two years in Jerusalem without seeing the king?

_____

_____

_____

2 Samuel 14:29

2. Why did Absalom send for Joab twice?

_____

_____

_____

2 Samuel 14:30

3. How did Absalom get Joab's attention when he refused to respond?

_____

_____

_____

2 Samuel 14:31–32

4. When Joab responded to the arson, why did Absalom say that he needed to speak with the king?

_____

_____

_____

David's Flight: Chapters 14:28–33 & 15

2 Samuel 14:33

5. How did David react to Absalom prostrating himself before him?

___

2 Samuel 15:1

6. What did Absalom provide for himself, and what did they represent?

___

2 Samuel 15:2–6

7. What did Absalom do to steal away the hearts of the men of Israel?

___

2 Samuel 15:7–9

8. What did Absalom ask permission to do, and what was his supposed purpose?

___

2 Samuel 15:10

9. What did Absalom do instead of going to the house of the Lord to worship?

___

2 Samuel 15:11–12

10. Whom did Absalom rally to his cause?

___

2 Samuel 15:13–14

11. When David heard that the men of Israel were behind Absalom becoming king, what did he decide to do?

___

2 Samuel 15:15–18

12. Why was leaving the city the best option for David and his people?

___

2 Samuel 15:19–21

13. What unlikely person followed David, and why?

___

___

___

2 Samuel 15:22

14. How did David respond to Ittai?

___

___

___

2 Samuel 15:23

15. Where did their "passing" lead them?

___

___

___

16. What was the significance of this wilderness?

___

___

___

2 Samuel 15:24

17. What did Zadok and the Levites attempt to carry out of Jerusalem?

___

___

___

2 Samuel 15:25–26

18. Why did David command them to return the ark to the city?

_____
_____
_____

2 Samuel 15:27–28

19. Why did David tell Zadok to remain in Jerusalem with the ark?

_____
_____
_____

2 Samuel 15:29–30

20. In what manner did David leave Jerusalem?

_____
_____
_____

2 Samuel 15:31

21. Who did a messenger say was conspiring with Absalom?

_____
_____
_____

22. Why was this man dangerous to David?

_____
_____
_____

DAVID'S FLIGHT: CHAPTERS 14:28–33 & 15

23. What did David pray would happen to his counsel?

2 Samuel 15:32–34

24. When Hushai the Archite came to the summit to meet David, David turned him back to the city. What command did he give the man?

2 Samuel 15:35–37

25. To whom was Hushai to report everything, who would then send word to David?

DISCUSSION QUESTIONS

1. Why did Absalom choose Hebron as the place to announce his coup?

2. David recognized that the Lord was bringing discipline upon him by removing him from the city. Why didn't David want the ark of the Lord with him in the wilderness?

2 SAMUEL

3. How does David's prayer to turn Ahithophel's counsel into foolishness reveal a heart change in David?

_____

_____

_____

DIGGING DEEPER (OPTIONAL)

Should you choose to dig deeper, complete the following Digging Deeper section.

In the lined note-taking spaces provided below, record what you observe in each passage and the questions you have about it.

Things to look for:

- Who is speaking?
- To whom is he speaking?
- What does this passage say about God, about Jesus, about the church, and about individual believers?
- What do readers of this text stand to gain?

Scripture Passages:

1 Kings 1:5–6

Matthew 12:46–50

Matthew 19:29

Mark 10:29–30

Philippians 4:6–7

Romans 8:31–39

Acts 1:1–11

Matthew 28:16–20

2 Corinthians 5:18–21

OBSERVATIONS

QUESTIONS

2 Samuel

A Little Deeper…

1. In what ways might we be tempted to place our relationships with family members, romantic partners, friends, neighbors, and colleagues over obedience to God? What did Jesus say our priority should be?

2. When faced with difficulties, what should our first response be? How can we exercise reliance on God over reliance on ourselves and worldly resources?

3. What are believers supposed to be doing in the time between the King's departure and His return?

SESSIONS 16–17

David's Flight, Continued: Chapters 16 & 17

Read 2 Samuel 16 & 17.

TOPIC OVERVIEW

- Ziba's manipulation of David
- David's harassment while in exile from Jerusalem
- Hushai's cunning counsel

LEARNING GOALS

- Understand the significance of acknowledging God's sovereignty.
- Identify points of humility in David's acceptance of God's discipline.
- Observe Absalom's pride and arrogance as he assumed the throne in Jerusalem.

2 Samuel

Core Questions

Background

1. By leaving the ark in Jerusalem, against normal patterns of kings, what was David effectively saying about where his power originated from?

_____

_____

_____

2. How did David's acknowledgment of God's sovereignty during his exile contribute to subsequent events?

_____

_____

_____

Answer the following questions as you watch and listen to the teaching.

2 Samuel 16:1–2

3. Mephibosheth's servant, Ziba, met David beyond the summit with gifts of donkeys, bread, raisins, fruit, and wine. Why did Ziba say he was presenting them to David?

_____

_____

_____

2 Samuel 16:3

4. What lie did Ziba tell him about Mephibosheth?

_____

_____

_____

DAVID'S FLIGHT, CONTINUED: CHAPTERS 16 & 17

2 Samuel 16:4

5. How did David respond, which perfectly played into Ziba's plan?

___

2 Samuel 16:5–6

6. Who came out to David in Bahurim, and what did he do?

___

2 Samuel 16:7–8

7. What curses did Shimei yell at David as he passed by?

___

2 Samuel 16:9–11

8. Abishai came to David's side and asked for permission to kill Shimei. What was David's response?

___

2 Samuel 16:12–13

9. What was David hoping for in allowing the man to continue cursing him?

2 Samuel 16:14

10. Where did David and his men hide out while Absalom entered Jerusalem, and for what reason?

2 Samuel 16:15–16

11. As soon as Absalom entered Jerusalem, what did Hushai do to gain Absalom's trust?

2 Samuel 16:17–19

12. When Absalom questioned why Hushai did not follow David into exile, what was his response?

DAVID'S FLIGHT, CONTINUED: CHAPTERS 16 & 17

2 Samuel 16:20–22

13. What counsel did Ahithophel first give to Absalom?

_____
_____
_____

2 Samuel 16:23

14. What was Ahithophel's authority in both David's and Absalom's courts?

_____
_____
_____

2 Samuel 17:1

15. What did Ahithophel ask Absalom's permission to do?

_____
_____
_____

2 Samuel 17:2–4

16. How did Ahithophel propose to defeat David?

_____
_____
_____

2 Samuel 17:5–6

17. Why did Absalom invite Hushai to give his opinion on the plan of attack?

_____

_____

_____

2 Samuel 17:7–8

18. What was Hushai's response to Absalom, and why did he say that Ahithophel's advice was not good?

_____

_____

_____

2 Samuel 17:9–10

19. Where did Hushai say that David would likely go to spend the night?

_____

_____

_____

2 Samuel 17:11–13

20. What was Hushai's suggested plan of attack for Absalom?

_____

_____

_____

DAVID'S FLIGHT, CONTINUED: CHAPTERS 16 & 17

2 Samuel 17:14

21. What was the ultimate reason Absalom listened to Hushai's advice instead of Ahithophel's?

_____

_____

_____

2 Samuel 17:15–16

22. To whom did Hushai tell the plan of attack, and what was the purpose?

_____

_____

_____

2 Samuel 17:17

23. Who were the spies who went to tell David the plans Hushai had relayed through a maidservant?

_____

_____

_____

2 Samuel 17:18–20

24. After a boy spotted Jonathan and Ahimaaz leaving, he ran and told Absalom. Where did the men hide to avoid capture?

_____

_____

_____

2 Samuel 17:21–22

25. What would David's escape inevitably mean for Absalom?

_____
_____
_____

2 Samuel 17:23

26. Knowing that he had betrayed God's anointed and David's escape would mean his inevitable death, what did Ahithophel do?

_____
_____
_____

2 Samuel 17:24

27. Where did David go before Absalom crossed the Jordan?

_____
_____
_____

Discussion Questions

1. What four points of comparison exist between David's flight and Christ's departure after His first coming?

_____
_____
_____

DAVID'S FLIGHT, CONTINUED: CHAPTERS 16 & 17

2. What was David's chief weakness as a leader and king? What was he lacking?

___

3. Shimei wrongly blamed David for killing Saul and Abner. How did David take his chastisement?

___

4. What was significant about the location where Absalom chose to take advantage of David's concubines?

___

5. What lesson for followers of Christ regarding spiritual warfare can be gleaned from Hushai's cunning?

___

DIGGING DEEPER (OPTIONAL)

Should you choose to dig deeper, complete the following Digging Deeper section.

In the lined note-taking spaces provided below, record what you observe in each passage and the questions you have about it.

Things to look for:

- Who is speaking?
- To whom is he speaking?
- What does this passage say about God, about Jesus, about the church, and about individual believers?
- What do readers of this text stand to gain?

Scripture Passages:

Matthew 10:16

Ephesians 6:10–18

1 Kings 3:3–15

Proverbs 2

Philippians 1:9–11

1 Corinthians 2:14–16

OBSERVATIONS

_____
_____
_____
_____
_____
_____
_____
_____
_____

Questions

A Little Deeper...

1. What does it mean for followers of Christ to "be shrewd as serpents and innocent as doves" (Matthew 10:16)?

2. What practical forms might this principle take? Have you ever seen or experienced it in action? How can you prepare yourself to put it into practice?

_____

_____

_____

3. What role does discernment play in the Christian walk, and how do we obtain it?

_____

_____

_____

SESSION 18

The Downfall of Absalom:
Chapters 17:24–29; 18; & 19:1–7

Read 2 Samuel 17:24–29; 18; & 19:1–7.

TOPIC OVERVIEW

- David's preparation for battle
- Absalom's death
- David's mourning for his son

LEARNING GOALS

- Identify Absalom's pride as his ultimate downfall.
- Observe David's incorrect priorities as he mourned for his son while the nation should have been rejoicing.

CORE QUESTIONS

Answer the following questions as you watch and listen to the teaching.

2 Samuel 17:24

1. Although the land God gave Israel spanned both east and west of the Jordan River, what did the Jews believe crossing the Jordan meant?

_____

_____

_____

2 Samuel 17:25

2. Whom did Absalom appoint as commander of his army in place of Joab? What was significant about this choice?

_____

_____

_____

2 Samuel 17:26–29

3. As Absalom camped in the land of Gilead, what did David's allies bring for his people?

_____

_____

_____

2 Samuel 18:1–2

4. How did David divide his fighting men to prepare for battle?

_____

_____

_____

THE DOWNFALL OF ABSALOM: CHAPTERS 17:24–29; 18; & 19:1–7

5. What was the valiant proposal that David made to his fighting men?

_____

_____

_____

2 Samuel 18:3–4

6. What was the people's response to David, and what did they say David was worth?

_____

_____

_____

2 Samuel 18:5

7. What were David's instructions to his commanders regarding Absalom?

_____

_____

_____

2 Samuel 18:6–8

8. What was the outcome of the battle, and how many men died?

_____

_____

_____

2 Samuel 18:9

9. How did Absalom become trapped in a tree?

_____

_____

_____

2 Samuel 18:10–11

10. When a messenger told Joab that he saw Absalom hanging, how did Joab respond?

_____

_____

_____

2 Samuel 18:12–13

11. How was the soldier correct in refraining from killing Absalom?

_____

_____

_____

2 Samuel 18:14–15

12. What did Joab do after hearing the soldier's report?

_____

_____

_____

2 Samuel 18:16

13. Why did Joab call off the pursuit of the Israelite people after Absalom's death?

_____

_____

_____

THE DOWNFALL OF ABSALOM: CHAPTERS 17:24–29; 18; & 19:1–7

2 Samuel 18:17–18

14. How did Joab and the men dispose of Absalom's body?

15. What was significant about this burial?

2 Samuel 18:19–20

16. Why did Ahimaaz so desperately want to run and tell David the result of the battle?

17. Why did Joab deny him the opportunity to convey the message?

2 Samuel 18:21–23

18. Whom did Joab appoint to tell the king of his son's death, and why did he choose him?

19. What did Ahimaaz say when he insisted on going with him?

___

2 Samuel 18:24–27

20. Why did David consider the men running by themselves to be good news?

___

2 Samuel 18:28–30

21. What news did Ahimaaz bring to David?

___

22. Why did Ahimaaz lie to the king?

___

2 Samuel 18:31–32

23. How did the Cushite deliver the news of Absalom's death to the king?

___

THE DOWNFALL OF ABSALOM: CHAPTERS 17:24–29; 18; & 19:1–7

2 Samuel 18:33

24. What emotional response did David have to the messengers' reports?

2 Samuel 19:1–2

25. What did David's mourning cause the nation to do?

2 Samuel 19:3–4

26. How did the soldiers return from battle, and how was this different from how they should have returned?

2 Samuel 19:5

27. How did Joab chastise David for his public mourning?

2 Samuel 19:6

28. How did Joab wisely describe David's action of mourning?

_____
_____
_____

2 Samuel 19:7

29. What was Joab's final, bold demand to the king?

_____
_____
_____

DISCUSSION QUESTIONS

1. What are some subtle cues in chapter 18 that reinforce that David, not Absalom, was king?

_____
_____
_____

2. Why did David's people insist that he stay away from the battle?

_____
_____
_____

3. While mercy and kindness are virtues, when do they do more harm than good?

_____
_____
_____

THE DOWNFALL OF ABSALOM: CHAPTERS 17:24–29; 18; & 19:1–7

4. How was it that more of Absalom's men died in the forest as they were running from the battle than in the battle itself?

_____

_____

_____

5. What did David's mourning over Absalom show to the people?

_____

_____

_____

DIGGING DEEPER (OPTIONAL)

Should you choose to dig deeper, complete the following Digging Deeper section.

In the lined note-taking spaces provided below, record what you observe in each passage and the questions you have about it.

Things to look for:

- Who is speaking?
- To whom is he speaking?
- What does this passage say about God, about Jesus, about the church, and about individual believers?
- What do readers of this text stand to gain?

Scripture Passages:

Proverbs 16:1–9

Proverbs 27:1

James 4:13–16

Psalm 10:2–4

2 Samuel

Habakkuk 2:4

Proverbs 18:12

Proverbs 29:23

Matthew 23:12

Ephesians 6:1–4

Deuteronomy 21:18–21

Proverbs 19:18–20

Proverbs 22:6

Proverbs 3:11–12

OBSERVATIONS

The Downfall of Absalom: Chapters 17:24–29; 18; & 19:1–7

QUESTIONS

A LITTLE DEEPER…

1. How do you tend to react when life doesn't go according to your plans? How can we honor God and acknowledge His sovereignty as we make plans for our days, weeks, months, and years?

2. How does God view human pride, and why is it sin? When have you experienced pride before a fall, and what did God teach you through that situation?

3. What place does discipline have in the Christian household today? How should Christian parents undertake the discipline of their children?

_____

_____

_____

SESSION 19

Reinstated as King: Chapter 19

Read 2 Samuel 19.

TOPIC OVERVIEW

- The restoration of David's reputation
- David's forgiveness of repentant rebels
- David's reinstatement as king in Jerusalem

LEARNING GOALS

- Understand the importance of humility when leading God's people.
- Identify acts of mercy and forgiveness in David's actions.

CORE QUESTIONS

Background

1. How did David's actions in mourning for his son shame his people?

_____

_____

_____

2. Joab's chastisement of David revealed what David had become as a father and a king. What is the basic principle of biblical leadership reflected in David's shortcomings?

_____

_____

_____

Answer the following questions as you watch and listen to the teaching.

2 Samuel 19:8

3. What was David's response to Joab's demands?

_____

_____

_____

2 Samuel 19:9–10

4. What were the main points of confusion among the tribes of Israel?

_____

_____

_____

2 Samuel 19:11–12

5. What were David's intentions in addressing the house of Judah?

_____

_____

_____

Reinstated as King: Chapter 19

2 Samuel 19:13

6. Why did David replace Joab with Amasa as commander?

_____

_____

_____

2 Samuel 19:14–15

7. How did Judah respond to David's message?

_____

_____

_____

2 Samuel 19:16–17

8. Who came to meet the king, along with the tribe of Judah?

_____

_____

_____

2 Samuel 19:18–20

9. Who fell at David's feet, and what was his plea?

_____

_____

_____

2 Samuel 19:21

10. Many of those around David objected to the prospect of showing forgiveness. What did Abishai say to the king?

_____

_____

_____

2 Samuel 19:22–23

11. What was David's Christlike response to Shimei?

_____

_____

_____

2 Samuel 19:24

12. Why did Mephibosheth come out to David in such an unkempt manner?

_____

_____

_____

2 Samuel 19:25–26

13. When David asked Mephibosheth why he didn't go with him, what was his reason?

_____

_____

_____

REINSTATED AS KING: CHAPTER 19

2 Samuel 19:27–28

14. Mephibosheth told David that Ziba had lied about him, but because he started with nothing, what did he leave to David's wise counsel?

___

2 Samuel 19:29

15. Surprisingly, what was David's reaction to discovering Ziba's deception?

___

2 Samuel 19:30

16. What was Mephibosheth's response to this? What did he want more than anything else?

___

2 Samuel 19:31–32

17. Who supported David during his exile?

___

2 Samuel 19:33

18. What kindness did David extend to Barzillai for taking care of him and his men?

_____

_____

_____

2 Samuel 19:34–36

19. What were Barzillai's reasons for refusing David's offer?

_____

_____

_____

2 Samuel 19:37–38

20. What did Barzillai suggest instead that David wholeheartedly agreed to do?

_____

_____

_____

2 Samuel 19:39–41

21. As David crossed over with the people of Judah and his followers, the other tribes came to greet him. What did they immediately start complaining about?

_____

_____

_____

REINSTATED AS KING: CHAPTER 19

2 Samuel 19:42–43

22. In a comical way, the tribes argued over whose idea it was to bring the king back home. How is this ironic when we consider how David left to go into exile?

___

DISCUSSION QUESTIONS

1. What prophetic picture do we see in the events of David's exile and return?

___

2. What four representative families who embrace the return of Jesus are mentioned in Zechariah 12?

___

3. Whom does Shimei represent in Jesus' return?

___

4. Why was Mephibosheth fine with Ziba having the entirety of his estate?

___

165

DIGGING DEEPER (OPTIONAL)

Should you choose to dig deeper, complete the following Digging Deeper section.

In the lined note-taking spaces provided below, record what you observe in each passage and the questions you have about it.

Things to look for:

- Who is speaking?
- To whom is he speaking?
- What does this passage say about God, about Jesus, about the church, and about individual believers?
- What do readers of this text stand to gain?

Scripture Passages:

James 2:13

Matthew 6:9–15

Matthew 19:16–22

Matthew 6:19–21, 24–34

Philippians 3:7–11

Romans 12:9–13

OBSERVATIONS

_____

_____

_____

_____

_____

Questions

2 Samuel

A Little Deeper...

1. When in your life have you chosen judgment or revenge over mercy? What were the immediate and long-term results? As Christians, why, when, and how should we extend mercy to other people?

_____
_____
_____

2. Mephibosheth understood that being a friend of the king was more important than worldly possessions. In what ways do his belief and attitude parallel what ours should be as Christians?

_____
_____
_____

3. What outlook and practices will help us to obtain the greatest benefits out of difficult circumstances?

_____
_____
_____

SESSION 20

Sheba's Rebellion: Chapter 20

Read 2 Samuel 20.

TOPIC OVERVIEW

- The pursuit of Sheba
- A wise woman who saves her city

LEARNING GOALS

- Identify the effects that bitterness can have in the hearts of men.
- Understand how a wise heart that follows God is stronger than a vengeful leader.

CORE QUESTIONS

Background

1. Why did the men of Israel and Judah argue at the banks of the Jordan River, according to 2 Samuel 19?

_____

_____

_____

2. What would these arguments eventually lead to in 1 Kings 12?

Answer the following questions as you watch and listen to the teaching.

2 Samuel 20:1–2

3. What did Sheba do that drove a wedge further into the division of the people?

2 Samuel 20:3

4. What did David do when he first returned to his house?

5. Why was this act significant?

Sheba's Rebellion: Chapter 20

2 Samuel 20:4

6. After David took care of his concubines, what did he summon Amasa, the new commander, to do?

_____
_____
_____

2 Samuel 20:5–6

7. When Amasa delayed longer than the appointed time, what was David's follow-up plan?

_____
_____
_____

2 Samuel 20:7

8. David sent Abishai to pursue Sheba, but who went after him? How did the military authority shift when he did?

_____
_____
_____

2 Samuel 20:8

9. Whom did Joab catch up to in his pursuit of Sheba?

_____
_____
_____

2 Samuel 20:9–10

10. What did Joab do as he got close to Amasa?

_____

_____

_____

2 Samuel 20:11

11. One of Joab's men stood beside Amasa and made a declaration to the troops. Why was his statement so important?

_____

_____

_____

2 Samuel 20:12

12. What was the solution for the troops being distracted by Amasa's mangled body?

_____

_____

_____

2 Samuel 20:13–14

13. How far did the army travel to pursue Sheba in the north?

_____

_____

_____

SHEBA'S REBELLION: CHAPTER 20

2 Samuel 20:15

14. What were Joab and his men doing in an attempt to get to Sheba?

_____

_____

_____

2 Samuel 20:16–17

15. Who requested to speak with Joab, and was this typical for cities to do?

_____

_____

_____

2 Samuel 20:18–19

16. What was the woman's appeal to Joab?

_____

_____

_____

2 Samuel 20:20–22

17. Was Joab's main purpose in the attack to destroy the city and the inheritance of the Lord? What was his goal?

_____

_____

_____

2 SAMUEL

16. What was the woman's response? Did it appease Joab?

_____

_____

_____

2 Samuel 20:23–26

17. As David's administrators are listed, who is named instead of Abishai as being over the whole army of Israel?

_____

_____

_____

DISCUSSION QUESTIONS

1. Why was blowing the shofar significant when Sheba made his declaration?

_____

_____

_____

2. Why was David unable to be with his concubines after Absalom's treachery?

_____

_____

_____

3. Why was it crucial for David to get to Sheba as quickly as possible?

_____

_____

_____

SHEBA'S REBELLION: CHAPTER 20

4. What are two potential reasons Joab killed Amasa?

_____

_____

_____

DIGGING DEEPER (OPTIONAL)

Should you choose to dig deeper, complete the following Digging Deeper section.

In the lined note-taking spaces provided below, record what you observe in each passage and the questions you have about it.

Things to look for:

- Who is speaking?
- To whom is he speaking?
- What does this passage say about God, about Jesus, about the church, and about individual believers?
- What do readers of this text stand to gain?

Scripture Passages:

Genesis 11:1–9

Matthew 20:20–28

Philippians 2:3–11

Psalm 127:1–2

Psalm 27:14

2 Samuel

Observations

Questions

A Little Deeper...

1. How does God view human ambition?

_____

_____

_____

2. How do the principles of God's kingdom differ from the principles of the world and human culture when it comes to advancement and position?

_____

_____

_____

3. How can we represent Christ's humility in our careers, ministry, and relationships?

_____

_____

_____

2 Samuel

SESSION 21

Biblical Justice: Chapter 21:1–14

Read 2 Samuel 21:1–14.

TOPIC OVERVIEW

- Famine in the land
- Making restitution
- Rizpah's grief and mourning

LEARNING GOALS

- Understand the significance of God's people being held responsible for the sins of Saul and his household.
- Identify David's act of mercy toward Rizpah.

CORE QUESTIONS

Background

1. How did Sheba sow division between Judah and Israel?

_____

_____

_____

2 SAMUEL

2. Who was originally in charge of the troops sent to gather the men of Judah before Joab regained control?

_____
_____
_____

Answer the following questions as you watch and listen to the teaching.

2 Samuel 21:1

3. What was occurring in the land that caused David to seek the presence of the Lord?

_____
_____
_____

4. What did God say was the reason the land was enduring hardship?

_____
_____
_____

2 Samuel 21:2–3

5. What did David do to try to rectify the situation?

_____
_____
_____

BIBLICAL JUSTICE: CHAPTER 21:1–14

2 Samuel 21:4

6. What did the Gibeonites say they had no desire for regarding restitution?

___

___

___

2 Samuel 21:5–6

7. What did the people request of the king, as payment for Saul's crimes? Which law did the Gibeonites apply in this request?

___

___

___

2 Samuel 21:7

8. Who among Saul's line did David spare, and why?

___

___

___

2 Samuel 21:8–9

9. Where were the men from Saul's household put to death? Why was this location significant?

___

___

___

2 Samuel 21:10

10. What did Rizpah, Aiah's daughter, do after the men were killed?

_____

_____

_____

2 Samuel 21:11–12

11. What did David do in response to Rizpah's actions?

_____

_____

_____

12. Why were Saul's and Jonathan's bones located in Jabesh-gilead?

_____

_____

_____

2 Samuel 21:13–14

13. How was David merciful to Rizpah after Saul and Jonathan's bones were gathered?

_____

_____

_____

14. What was God's response to this act of justice and mercy?

_____

_____

_____

BIBLICAL JUSTICE: CHAPTER 21:1–14

DISCUSSION QUESTIONS

1. How was a covenant established between Israel and the Gibeonites?

_____

_____

_____

2. Why did Joshua fall for the Gibeonites' trickery?

_____

_____

_____

3. Why did David need to make atonement for the Gibeonites?

_____

_____

_____

4. Why did Rizpah remain with the hung bodies?

_____

_____

_____

DIGGING DEEPER (OPTIONAL)

Should you choose to dig deeper, complete the following Digging Deeper section.

In the lined note-taking spaces provided below, record what you observe in each passage and the questions you have about it.

Things to look for:

- Who is speaking?
- To whom is he speaking?

2 SAMUEL

- What does this passage say about God, about Jesus, about the church, and about individual believers?
- What do readers of this text stand to gain?

Scripture Passages:

2 Corinthians 12:9–10

Psalm 46:1–3

Jonah 2:1–2

Exodus 3:7–8

Psalm 116:2

Revelation 11:3–5

Judges 7:7–14, 20–23

Genesis 14:18–20

Numbers 24:16

Deuteronomy 32:8

Psalm 9:3

Exodus 19:16

2 Timothy 3:16

Psalm 23:4

Deuteronomy 6:1–3, 10–19

Observations

Questions

A LITTLE DEEPER...

1. How was God's power shown in David's weakness, as Paul described in 2 Corinthians 12:9?

_____

_____

_____

2. What is the fate, in the end, of all who stand against God and His plan (Revelation 11)?

_____

_____

_____

3. Israel often crushed her enemies with military numbers that did not make sense. What is one example of this, found in Judges 7?

_____

_____

_____

SESSION 22A

"The Horn of My Salvation": Chapters 21:15–22 & 22:1–20

Read 2 Samuel 21:15–22 & 22:1–20.

Topic Overview

- David's removal from battle due to his worth
- The Lord's deliverance

Learning Goals

- Gain a clearer picture of David's worth to the kingdom of Israel.
- Identify times of deliverance from the Lord.
- Understand the awe-inspiring nature of a wrathful God.

Core Questions

Answer the following questions as you watch and listen to the teaching.

2 Samuel 21:15

1. What does "David became weary" mean in this text?

_____
_____
_____

2 Samuel 21:16

2. How was the enemy in this battle reminiscent of Goliath, whom David fought in his youth?

_____
_____
_____

2 Samuel 21:17

3. Who helped David and struck down the giant? What did he tell David?

_____
_____
_____

2 Samuel 21:18–22

4. Time and again, David and his men defeated the Philistines and the giants among them. How did God demonstrate His power through weakness in David's battles?

_____
_____
_____

"The Horn of My Salvation": Chapter 21:15–22 & 22:1–20

2 Samuel 22:1–2

5. When did David speak or sing the song recorded here?

_____

_____

_____

2 Samuel 22:3–4

6. From what did David credit God for saving him?

_____

_____

_____

2 Samuel 22:5–6

7. What four things did David say were scaring or ensnaring him?

_____

_____

_____

2 Samuel 22:7

8. What did David do in his distress, and what was God's response?

_____

_____

_____

2 Samuel 22:8–9

9. How was the earth affected by the Lord's anger?

_____

_____

_____

2 Samuel 22:10–11

10. How did the Lord come down from heaven?

_____

_____

_____

2 Samuel 22:12–14

11. What elements of nature did David use to describe the Lord's descent from heaven?

_____

_____

_____

2 Samuel 22:15–16

12. What did the Lord use to scatter David's enemies?

_____

_____

_____

13. What natural effects did the Lord's rebuke have on the world?

_____

_____

_____

2 Samuel 22:17–18

14. How did the Lord rescue David after rebuking his enemies?

___

2 Samuel 22:19–20

15. What did David say was the reason the Lord rescued him?

___

DISCUSSION QUESTIONS

1. Why was David told not to go into battle anymore?

___

2. In the first few verses of 2 Samuel 22, how can we see that David had an intimate relationship with God?

___

3. In verse 6, to what does the word *Sheol* refer?

___

4. How does Jonah's prayer in Jonah 2 compare to David's song of the Lord's deliverance?

_____

_____

_____

5. The Lord rescued David because the Lord delighted in him (2 Samuel 22:20). What does the word *delighted* mean in the original language of the text?

_____

_____

_____

DIGGING DEEPER (OPTIONAL)

Should you choose to dig deeper, complete the following Digging Deeper section.

In the lined note-taking spaces provided below, record what you observe in each passage and the questions you have about it.

Things to look for:

- Who is speaking?
- To whom is he speaking?
- What does this passage say about God, about Jesus, about the church, and about individual believers?
- What do readers of this text stand to gain?

Scripture Passages:

Genesis 15:4–6

Colossians 1:21–22

1 John 1:9

1 John 2:1

Psalm 27:1–6

Psalm 18:30

Isaiah 40:28

Psalm 46:1

Ephesians 6:16–17

Psalm 110:1–2

OBSERVATIONS

_____
_____
_____
_____
_____
_____
_____
_____
_____
_____
_____
_____

QUESTIONS

_____
_____
_____

2 Samuel

A Little Deeper...

1. The vivid imagery of light and dark in 1 John 1:5–7 reminds us of a promise-keeping God. What is our hope when we struggle in sin?

2. In Ephesians 6, how did Paul describe the means of God's outworking power and grace to believers in Christ?

SESSION 22B

David's Praise to the Lord: Chapter 22:20–51

Read 2 Samuel 22:20–51.

Topic Overview

- Obedience of and faithfulness to the Lord
- How Yahweh rewards the faithful
- The excellence of the Lord experienced in the Lord

Learning Goals

- Identify points of humility in David's praise and worship.
- Understand the concept of reciprocity the Lord has for believers and unbelievers.

CORE QUESTIONS

2 Samuel 22:21–22

1. For what did David say the Lord rewarded him?

_____

_____

_____

2 Samuel 22:23–25

2. How was David made righteous and clean before a Holy God, even with his sinful acts and mistakes?

_____

_____

_____

3. Who else in the Old Testament was deemed righteous based on his belief? How was he granted righteousness?

_____

_____

_____

2 Samuel 22:26–27

4. What concept of holy reciprocity did David attribute to God?

_____

_____

_____

DAVID'S PRAISE TO THE LORD: CHAPTER 22:20–51

5. How is this same reciprocity seen in reverse for those who are not believers?

_____
_____
_____

2 Samuel 22:28

6. Whom does the Lord rescue? Whom is He against?

_____
_____
_____

2 Samuel 22:29–30

7. What help did the Lord provide to David?

_____
_____
_____

2 Samuel 22:31–32

8. On what attribute of God did David focus in these verses?

_____
_____
_____

2 Samuel 22:33

9. How is one seen as blameless before God? Whose efforts achieve this righteousness?

_____

_____

_____

2 Samuel 22:34–35

10. How did the Lord prepare David to win against his enemies?

_____

_____

_____

2 Samuel 22:36–37

11. What measures of protection did the Lord give to David throughout his life?

_____

_____

_____

2 Samuel 22:38–39

12. What did the Lord's help and provisions allow David to do?

_____

_____

_____

DAVID'S PRAISE TO THE LORD: CHAPTER 22:20–51

2 Samuel 22:40–41

13. Although David was mighty in battle, to whom did David attribute his victories?

_____

_____

_____

2 Samuel 22:42–43

14. What happened when David's enemies turned to the Lord for help?

_____

_____

_____

2 Samuel 22:44

15. Aside from his enemies, what else did David say the Lord delivered him from? How did this secure his kingship?

_____

_____

_____

2 Samuel 22:45–46

16. How did David's partnership with the Lord garner mercy from surrounding nations?

_____

_____

_____

2 Samuel 22:47–49

17. What was David ultimately saying when he proclaimed that the Lord lives?

_____

_____

_____

2 Samuel 22:50–51

18. Where and to whom did David announce his praises to the Lord?

_____

_____

_____

DISCUSSION QUESTIONS

1. In the Old Testament, salvation is connected to physical deliverance, whereas salvation in the New Testament is connected to spiritual deliverance (eternal security). How does Scripture interlink the outworking of salvation for both the Old and New Testament?

_____

_____

_____

2. David was deemed righteous because he trusted in the Lord's promises. How does Scripture define the New Testament believer as being deemed righteous?

_____

_____

_____

DAVID'S PRAISE TO THE LORD: CHAPTER 22:20–51

3. How does allowing the Lord to fight our battles give greater satisfaction than retaliation does?

_____

_____

_____

4. What protection is attributed to David that also shows itself in Ephesians 6?

_____

_____

_____

DIGGING DEEPER (OPTIONAL)

Should you choose to dig deeper, complete the following Digging Deeper section.

In the lined note-taking spaces provided below, record what you observe in each passage and the questions you have about it.

Things to look for:

- Who is speaking?
- To whom is he speaking?
- What does this passage say about God, about Jesus, about the church, and about individual believers?
- What do readers of this text stand to gain?

Scripture Passages:

2 Peter 1:20–21

John 5:39–40

2 Timothy 3:16–17

1 Kings 2:10

2 Samuel

Numbers 24:3–4, 15–17

Proverbs 30:1

Acts 2:29–31

1 Chronicles 17:10–12, 14, 16

Genesis 3:15; 4:1; 15:16; 22:17–18

Psalm 2

Psalm 22:1–5, 11–18, 27–28

Psalm 89:3–4, 19–29, 34–37

Psalm 110

Zechariah 6:11–13

Deuteronomy 18:9–14

Isaiah 7:14; 9:6–7; 40:3

Isaiah 53

Micah 5:2

Malachi 4:1–2

Matthew 23:39

2 Corinthians 1:20

Jeremiah 23:5

Jeremiah 37:4

Revelation 16:1; 17:14; 18:4–8; 19:1–3, 11–16

OBSERVATIONS

QUESTIONS

2 SAMUEL

A LITTLE DEEPER...

1. According to 2 Peter, how do we come by prophecy?

_____

_____

_____

2. How did David also operate as a prophet during his lifetime, as mentioned in Acts 2?

_____

_____

_____

3. How does Revelation 16–19 depict the second coming of Christ to an unbelieving world?

_____

_____

_____

SESSION 23A

David's Last Song: Chapter 23:1–7

Read 2 Samuel 23:1–7.

Topic Overview

- The subject of David's last song
- The Spirit's revelation
- A future King

Learning Goals

- Understand the translation differences that shift interpretation.
- Identify the prophecies regarding Christ.

Core Questions

Answer the following questions as you watch and listen to the teaching.

2 Samuel

2 Samuel 23:1

1. Since these were not David's final words before death, what should we understand "last words" to mean in this text?

_____
_____
_____

2. What four descriptors did the poet list in this verse, and at first, to whom do they seem to apply?

_____
_____
_____

3. Based on variations of translation in this verse alone, who is more likely the subject of David's final song to Israel?

_____
_____
_____

2 Samuel 23:2

4. Who did David say communicated through him to give an understanding of the future Messiah?

_____
_____
_____

DAVID'S LAST SONG: CHAPTER 23:1–7

2 Samuel 23:3–4

5. What did David say was the result of one ruling over people in righteousness?

_____
_____
_____

2 Samuel 23:5

6. What is David's first point regarding his household, based on further examination of other translations?

_____
_____
_____

7. With the proper Hebrew phrasing in translation, what does verse 5 say regarding God's promise?

_____
_____
_____

2 Samuel 23:6

8. What did David say will happen to the "worthless," or evil?

_____
_____
_____

2 Samuel 23:7

9. What were David's intentions in focusing on those who rejected the King?

_____

_____

_____

DISCUSSION QUESTIONS

1. What are the three main reasons for studying the Scriptures?

_____

_____

_____

2. How does Acts 2 compare David and Christ regarding their deaths?

_____

_____

_____

3. What are two requirements for an ideal king to rule in accordance with God's will?

_____

_____

_____

4. What four promises did the Lord tell David regarding his seed who would rule on his throne?

_____

_____

_____

DIGGING DEEPER (OPTIONAL)

Should you choose to dig deeper, complete the following Digging Deeper section.

In the lined note-taking spaces provided below, record what you observe in each passage and the questions you have about it.

Things to look for:

- Who is speaking?
- To whom is he speaking?
- What does this passage say about God, about Jesus, about the church, and about individual believers?
- What do readers of this text stand to gain?

Scripture Passages:

James 1:12

1 Corinthians 9:24

Psalm 18:25–27

Leviticus 25:23

Deuteronomy 32:43

Mark 14:3–9

1 Samuel 26:8–9, 15–16, 23–25

Matthew 25:17–30

Luke 12:48; 19:11–27

1 Kings 1:8; 2:25

2 Timothy 2:11–13

Observations

Questions

A LITTLE DEEPER…

1. What does James 1 teach regarding those who endure difficulty or trial?

___

2. What insights does Matthew 25 provide into the stewardship of talents and the faithfulness of God's servants?

___

3. What does Luke 12 say about those who have been entrusted with much?

___

2 Samuel

SESSION 23B

The Reward of Great Men: Chapter 23:8–39

Read 2 Samuel 23:8–39.

TOPIC OVERVIEW

- David's top three mighty men
- Famous acts of valor
- The result of disobedient actions

LEARNING GOALS

- Identify the mighty men David thought were worthy of recognition.
- Examine the cause of Joab's exclusion from the list.
- Explore David's heart of humility in his refusal to drink water from Bethlehem.

CORE QUESTIONS

Background

1. To whom was David referring as the ideal and future King of Israel?

_____

_____

_____

2 Samuel

2. What will the future King do once and for all?

___

Answer the following questions as you watch and listen to the teaching.

2 Samuel 23:8

3. According to the ranking of David's men, who was "chief" of the three?

___

4. How many was David's chief captain said to have killed at once?

___

2 Samuel 23:9–10

5. What notable achievement did Eleazar accomplish to earn him the rank of second among David's three mighty men?

___

6. What was significant about the fact that Eleazar fought with David against the Philistines?

___

THE REWARD OF GREAT MEN: CHAPTER 23:8–39

2 Samuel 23:11–12

7. Why was the plot of land that Shammah defended specifically mentioned?

_____
_____
_____

8. Why was this a demonstration of Shammah's great faith?

_____
_____
_____

2 Samuel 23:13–14

9. What other time in David's life was he in the cave of Adullam?

_____
_____
_____

2 Samuel 23:15

10. What was significant about David's craving?

_____
_____
_____

2 Samuel 23:16

11. What did the three mighty men do for David? What risk did they take?

_____
_____
_____

2 Samuel 23:17

12. What shocking response did David give in the face of their bravery and loyalty?

_____

_____

_____

2 Samuel 23:18–19

13. What did it mean that Abishai "had a name" along with the three?

_____

_____

_____

2 Samuel 23:20

14. What was the significance of Benaiah killing a lion in the middle of a pit on a snowy day?

_____

_____

_____

2 Samuel 23:21

15. Who else did Benaiah kill, and how?

_____

_____

_____

THE REWARD OF GREAT MEN: CHAPTER 23:8–39

2 Samuel 23:22–23

16. How did David honor Benaiah?

_____

_____

_____

2 Samuel 23:24–39

17. Why was Joab not mentioned among David's mighty men, even with Joab's many victories?

_____

_____

_____

DISCUSSION QUESTIONS

1. As believers, when do we receive our rewards?

_____

_____

_____

2. What did David mean in 2 Samuel 23:17 when he said, "Shall I drink the blood of the men who went in jeopardy of their lives?"

_____

_____

_____

2 Samuel

3. What story in Mark's Gospel is reminiscent of the pouring out of the water in light of a great potential sacrifice?

_____

_____

_____

4. After salvation, what is the next step for a believer in Christ?

_____

_____

_____

DIGGING DEEPER (OPTIONAL)

Should you choose to dig deeper, complete the following Digging Deeper section.

In the lined note-taking spaces provided below, record what you observe in each passage and the questions you have about it.

Things to look for:

- Who is speaking?
- To whom is he speaking?
- What does this passage say about God, about Jesus, about the church, and about individual believers?
- What do readers of this text stand to gain?

Scripture Passages:

James 1:13

1 Chronicles 21:1–5

Exodus 30:11–16

Numbers 1:1–4; 26:1–2

Proverbs 18:10–12

1 John 1:9

Micah 7:18

Jeremiah 18:8; 26:3

Amos 7:3, 6

Jonah 3:10

Mark 8:34–35

Matthew 6:21

Hebrews 9:22

OBSERVATIONS

QUESTIONS

_____
_____
_____
_____
_____
_____
_____
_____
_____
_____
_____
_____
_____

A LITTLE DEEPER...

1. What does the book of James say tempts a man to sin?

_____
_____
_____

2. Although no one is excluded from God's judgment, what does Micah 7:18 tell us that the Lord will do?

_____
_____
_____

THE REWARD OF GREAT MEN: CHAPTER 23:8–39

3. Where do our hearts reside, according to Matthew 6:21? What does this mean?

_____
_____
_____

2 Samuel

SESSION 24

Sin, Judgment, and Restoration: Chapter 24

Read 2 Samuel 24.

TOPIC OVERVIEW

- David's sin
- The demand for judgment
- The sending of a pestilence
- The restoration of fellowship

LEARNING GOALS

- Identify David's arrogance in relying on the size of his military.
- Understand the need for punishment and the extent of the Lord's mercy in response to David's sin.

CORE QUESTIONS

Answer the following questions as you watch and listen to the teaching.

2 Samuel 24:1

1. Who incited David to number the people of Israel? Why?

_____

_____

_____

2 Samuel 24:2

2. What was the root behind God's anger against Israel?

_____

_____

_____

3. What kind of census was this, since David did not command the women and children to be counted?

_____

_____

_____

2 Samuel 24:3

4. In response to David's command, what did Joab say the Lord was able to do?

_____

_____

_____

Sin, Judgment, and Restoration: Chapter 24

2 Samuel 24:4–8

5. How long did it take Joab and his men to complete the census?

_____
_____
_____

2 Samuel 24:9

6. How many fighting men were found in Israel and Judah?

_____
_____
_____

2 Samuel 24:10

7. Why was David's heart troubled after he numbered the people?

_____
_____
_____

8. What did David immediately do after he recognized his sin?

_____
_____
_____

2 Samuel 24:11–12

9. What did the Lord offer David through his court seer?

_____
_____
_____

2 Samuel 24:13

10. What were David's options for punishment?

___

2 Samuel 24:14

11. What was David's choice for punishment, and what was his reasoning?

___

2 Samuel 24:15

12. How many men died as a result of David's sin?

___

2 Samuel 24:16

13. How did the Lord demonstrate His control over the pestilence?

___

14. What was significant about the location where the angel of destruction stopped?

___

SIN, JUDGMENT, AND RESTORATION: CHAPTER 24

2 Samuel 24:17

15. What was David's response to the pestilence? Who did he say should be punished?

_____
_____
_____

16. What caused the Lord to relent?

_____
_____
_____

2 Samuel 24:18–19

17. What did the prophet tell David to do after his repentance, and where was he to build?

_____
_____
_____

2 Samuel 24:20

18. What did Araunah do when he saw the king coming toward him?

_____
_____
_____

2 Samuel 24:21

19. What did David tell Araunah he wanted to do, and for what purpose?

_____

_____

_____

2 Samuel 24:22–23

20. What did Araunah offer the king, free of charge?

_____

_____

_____

2 Samuel 24:24

21. What was the main reason David insisted on paying for the threshing floor?

_____

_____

_____

2 Samuel 24:25

22. After David built an altar and offered sacrifices to the Lord, how did the Lord respond?

_____

_____

_____

SIN, JUDGMENT, AND RESTORATION: CHAPTER 24

DISCUSSION QUESTIONS

1. Why did David believe it was better to endure pestilence than war as a punishment from God?

_____

_____

_____

2. Why did the Lord "relent" and stop the pestilence? Was David able to change God's mind?

_____

_____

_____

3. Why did Araunah say to David, "May the LORD your God accept you" (2 Samuel 24:23)?

_____

_____

_____

DIGGING DEEPER (OPTIONAL)

Should you choose to dig deeper, complete the following Digging Deeper section.

In the lined note-taking spaces provided below, record what you observe in each passage and the questions you have about it.

Things to look for:

- Who is speaking?
- To whom is he speaking?
- What does this passage say about God, about Jesus, about the church, and about individual believers?
- What do readers of this text stand to gain?

2 SAMUEL

Scripture Passages:

Proverbs 18:10–12

1 John 1:9

Jonah 3:10

OBSERVATIONS

QUESTIONS

SIN, JUDGMENT, AND RESTORATION: CHAPTER 24

_____
_____
_____
_____
_____

A LITTLE DEEPER...

1. Much like David's pridefulness in the size of his military, what does Proverbs 18 say is the precursor to the destruction of a man's heart?

_____
_____
_____

2. God always responds with justice and mercy, just as He relented from the pestilence on the land. How can we align our hearts to trust God with our lives, according to Joshua 1:9?

_____
_____
_____

3. The Lord relented from the disaster over the people of Israel once David repented. How is this same principle reflected in the story of Jonah?

_____
_____
_____

2 Samuel

APPENDIX

Answer Key

SESSION 1
DAVID MOURNS SAUL'S DEATH: CHAPTER 1

CORE QUESTIONS

Background

1. **Who wrote the book of Samuel, and why is this important to understand?** Samuel, the prophet, along with probably one or two other prophets, like Gad or Nathan, wrote the book. At many points, the author took care to show how events in David's life unfolded according to the will of God. This history was relayed from a perspective of absolute alignment with the will and commands of God.

2. **What were the main events that 1 Samuel covered?** The rise of kings in Israel and a rivalry between Israel's first king, Saul, and his successor, David.

3. **What is a major theme related to God in 1 and 2 Samuel? How is that theme portrayed in the recorded events of David's life?** David's story begins with the perspective of appreciation for God's sovereignty, and the events of his life are a testimony to this. The Lord worked patiently with David through his surrender to the will of God and his failures that left him having to work his way back into alignment with God's sovereign will.

2 Samuel 1:1

4. Where in Judah did David and his men remain for two days after defeating the Amalekites? What was the significance of this location? According to 1 Samuel 27:1–7, David found favor with the Philistine king, Achish, while David was fleeing Saul. The king gave him the country town of Ziklag as his own to live in. David then stayed in this town, which he already had control over, while he strategically prepared to become king.

2 Samuel 1:2

5. What is the significance of it being the third day when the messenger arrived at David's camp? It was a four-day journey on foot at a normal walking pace. The messenger would have had to run. He wanted to be the first to inform David. For the one who brought the news to David, there was an opportunity for a reward but also a great risk.

2 Samuel 1:3–4

6. Which two main characters did the messenger inform David were dead? Why was this important for David's future kingship? Saul and Jonathan were reported to be dead. Even though David had already been anointed king over Israel by Samuel, his path to kingship was clearer with both the king and his heir dead.

2 Samuel 1:5–7

7. Where was Saul when the messenger found him, and what was he doing? Why wasn't he successful? According to the messenger, Saul was on Mt. Gilboa, leaning on his spear (committing suicide). He wasn't successful due to his weakness. With his mortal wound, he wasn't strong enough to finish the job.

2 Samuel 1:8–10

8. What did the messenger do when Saul asked him to kill him, and what reason did the messenger give for doing so? He stood beside Saul and killed him, took his crown and bracelet as proof, and brought them to David. According to the messenger, Saul was already mortally wounded and destined to die, so he took Saul's life as an act of mercy.

ANSWER KEY

2 Samuel 1:11–12

9. What did David and his men do when the messenger relayed the news? They mourned, wept, and fasted until evening for Saul, Jonathan, and the men who had died in battle.

2 Samuel 1:13

10. Where was the messenger from, and why did it matter to David? What emboldened the servant to reveal his true ethnicity? The man was an Amalekite. Saul's failure to follow God's instructions to destroy all of the Amalekites and their possessions resulted in the loss of his dynasty to David. Furthermore, David had just returned from killing Amalekites. This particular man was born in Israel to an Amalekite immigrant. He expected being under the law to protect him, but since he had sinned according to the law, he was punished for his crime according to the law.

2 Samuel 1:14–16

11. What three things did David do when the messenger answered his question?

- David asked why the messenger wasn't afraid to kill the Lord's anointed.
- He had him killed by a soldier.
- He said that Saul's blood was on this man's head by his own testimony.

2 Samuel 1:17–18

12. How did David first mourn over Saul and Jonathan's deaths? What were the implications of their deaths? David wrote and chanted a song of lament called "The Song of the Bow." He then commanded it to be taught to the sons of Judah. Saul's and Jonathan's deaths made David's anointing as king even clearer and paved the way for him to become Israel's rightful leader. Saul was Israel's first king, and his death had a significant impact on Israel. Personally, Jonathan was David's closest friend, and his death would have affected David on a deeply personal level.

2 Samuel 1:19

13. What did David say to show his respect for Saul in this verse? Why did he choose those particular words? He said the nation's beauty had been slain on the high places. Since Saul was killed and disfigured on the high places of Mt. Gilboa, the nation and even the landscape had part of its beauty permanently altered.

2 Samuel 1:20

14. **Why did David not want the news of Saul's death to spread?** The Philistines were Israel's greatest enemy during this time, and David couldn't bear the thought of them celebrating Saul's death.

2 Samuel 1:21

15. **What did David pronounce over Gilboa, and why?** David essentially cursed the mountains of Gilboa since even the land had a part in the death of Saul.

2 Samuel 1:22–23

16. **What praises did David proclaim over Saul and Jonathan?** Neither one ran from the battle, and both defeated their enemies. Even in death, they were together. They were swifter than eagles and stronger than lions.

2 Samuel 1:24

17. **Why did David tell the daughters of Israel to lament Saul's passing? Why would this have been significant to the nation?** Saul was Israel's first king. Under his leadership, Israel became wealthy. Even though he failed, he fulfilled their desire for a leader and made them rich under his rule.

2 Samuel 1:25–27

18. **At the end of the lament, over whom did David mourn the most, and what long-term effects might this person's death have had on David's future decisions as king?** He mourned the most for Jonathan, his best friend. Jonathan was David's confidant, counselor, and even protector. Without this friendship, David would spiral many times into poor military and personal decisions.

Discussion Questions (Answers may vary.)

1. **A major theme in 1 and 2 Samuel is God's sovereignty. In what ways do we see God's sovereignty displayed in David's life?** God chose David out of a group of brothers who seemed more fit to rule. David started forming his reputation early

ANSWER KEY

when he slayed Goliath. He was faithful to God and didn't lay a hand on Saul, yet God still removed Saul from the throne to prepare a way for David to become king.

2. **What is historically significant about the messenger's place of origin?** He was an Amalekite. During Saul's reign, Saul failed to destroy all the Amalekites, as God instructed. This disobedience cost him his throne and lined David up for kingship.

3. **Even though he had multiple chances, why did David never attack Saul?** He knew that Saul was God's anointed king and God would dethrone Saul at the right time. If David had forced himself into Saul's position, that would have been disobeying God just as much as ignoring Him would have been.

4. **Do you think the messenger was telling the truth about being the one who killed Saul? Why or why not?** The details point to the possibility that the man was lying. According to 1 Samuel 31:2–6, Saul committed suicide unassisted. Saul and his armor-bearer, who refused to help Saul die, were found dead. It's possible that the messenger only witnessed this, or perhaps he assisted the king. However, it's unlikely that the armor-bearer would have watched someone else kill his king. The messenger was probably exploiting the king's death and hoping for a reward.

SESSION 2
DIVIDED KINGDOM, DIVIDED HEART: CHAPTERS 2:1–32 & 3:1–16

CORE QUESTIONS

2 Samuel 2:1

1. **When David asked the Lord if he should go to Judah, what was God's response, and where did He tell David to go? What was significant about this location in particular?** He told David to go to Hebron. It sat on the highest point in the land of Judah and offered a strategic advantage in warfare.

2 Samuel 2:2–3

2. **Whom did David take with him?** His two wives: Ahinoam the Jezreelitess, and Abigail, the widow of Nabal the Carmelite. He also brought his men who were with him.

2 Samuel 2:4

3. **What did the men of Judah do when David and his people settled into the cities?** They anointed him king over the house of Judah and told him that the men of Jabesh-gilead were the ones who buried Saul.

2 Samuel 2:5–7

4. **How did David respond when he heard who buried Saul? Why was this important to David?** He sent messengers to Jabesh-gilead to bless them and also to let them know that he was now king. He rewarded them because burying Saul showed honor to the Lord's anointed. Even though David was set up to be king, God had still chosen Saul, and the men showed respect for their fallen king by giving him a proper burial.

2 Samuel 2:8

5. **Who was Abner, and what did he do in response to David being anointed king?** Abner was the son of Ner and the commander of Saul's army. He took Saul's other son, Ish-bosheth, and brought him to Mahanaim.

2 Samuel 2:9

6. **What significant events took place in response to Abner's action?** Abner made Ish-bosheth king over Gilead, over the Ashurites, Jezreel, Ephraim, Benjamin, and all of Israel. Since Saul and Jonathan were dead, Ish-bosheth would have been considered next in line for the throne.

2 Samuel 2:10

7. **Whom did the house of Judah follow? How was the nation divided politically?** They followed David and named him their king. The nation was divided: the northern tribes followed their newly appointed king, Ish-bosheth, while southern Judah followed their new king, David.

2 Samuel 2:11

8. **How long did David reign over the house of Judah? How long was Ish-bosheth's reign?** David reigned for seven years and six months. Ish-bosheth reigned for two years.

ANSWER KEY

2 Samuel 2:12–13

9. **Who met at the pool of Gibeon, and what were their allegiances?** Abner and Ish-bosheth's army met Joab and David's army at the pool of Gibeon. Abner was in alliance with Ish-bosheth and loyal to the house of Saul, serving as the commander of Saul's army. Joab was the commander of David's army and loyal to David and the house of Judah.

2 Samuel 2:14–15

10. **What was the proposal for this attempted peace treaty? Why would they have proposed such a battle?** They proposed that young men should fight in hand-to-hand combat to the death. Abner's idea was to pit the men against each other as a way of predicting who would win the battle. The winning side would claim the right to rule all the tribes.

2 Samuel 2:16–17

11. **What was the result of the battle?** After each side unexpectedly killed the other, resulting in every contestant's death, the two delegations fought. David's forces, led by Joab, gained the upper hand in the battle and began to chase Abner and his forces.

2 Samuel 2:18

12. **Who were the three brothers present at the battle?** Joab, Abishai, and Asahel.

2 Samuel 2:19–20

13. **Who pursued Abner, and what was his greatest skill?** Asahel pursued Abner instead of the other men. Asahel was known for being an extremely fast runner.

2 Samuel 2:21–22

14. **What did Abner try to convince Asahel to do, and why?** He tried to convince Asahel to fight one of the other men and even take his spoil. Abner knew that he would easily defeat Asahel and didn't want to kill him.

2 Samuel 2:23

15. **What was Asahel's fate?** Asahel refused to attack anyone else, so Abner struck him with the butt end of his spear. Asahel's speed in running caused him to become impaled on the spear, and he died.

16. **What were the possible reasons for Abner using the butt end of his spear?** This could have been to try to avoid killing Asahel, meaning only to injure him, or it could have been out of cruelty, to cause a more painful death with the blunt end.

2 Samuel 2:24–25

17. **Where did Joab and Abishai finally catch up with Abner?** The hill of Ammah, in front of Giah by the way of the wilderness of Gibeon.

18. **Who rallied behind Abner? Why did they side with him?** The sons of Benjamin sided with Abner. They were in the northern territory of Israel and were one of the tribes that Ish-bosheth ruled. Also, Joab was pursuing Abner northward into the territory of Benjamin, which made it a strategic place for them to support Abner's army.

2 Samuel 2:26–27

19. **Who was ultimately to blame for the battle?** Even though Abner tried to blame Joab for not calling off his men, Joab correctly reminded Abner that he was the one who called for the contest. Abner was to blame for the bloodshed.

2 Samuel 2:28

20. **Why did Joab blow the trumpet to stop the pursuit of Israel?** Joab knew that he couldn't defeat Abner under the current circumstances. Better to retreat and live to fight another day than risk losing more men.

2 Samuel 2:29

21. **Where did Abner and his men return after the battle? What made this location significant?** They returned to Mahanaim. It was the place where Jacob had met two angels of the Lord (Genesis 32:2).

ANSWER KEY

2 Samuel 2:30–31

22. **How many men from each side were killed?** David's delegation lost a total of twenty men. Abner lost 360.

2 Samuel 2:32

23. **Where did Joab bury Asahel?** Asahel was buried in the family tomb in Bethlehem.

2 Samuel 3:1

24. **What was the long-term result of Abner's ill-advised combat? What was the ultimate outcome of the long war between the houses of Saul and David?** The conflict turned into a long war between the north and the south. However, every battle strengthened David's side while the house of Saul grew weaker.

2 Samuel 3:2–5

25. **Who were the children born to David at Hebron?** His firstborn was Amnon, then Chileab, Absalom, Adonijah, Shephatiah, and Ithream.

26. **Although unlawful by God's command, David had many wives. What is the most likely reason most of the marriages were made?** Although the Lord outlawed marrying for political advantage in Deuteronomy 7:3, many of David's marriages were probably made to establish political alliances to shore up his power in the land.

2 Samuel 3:6–7

27. **How was Abner making himself strong in the house of Saul? Why was this considered a power play?** Abner slept with one of Saul's concubines. By claiming one of the royal concubines as his own, he was stealing the right to produce heirs to the throne.

28. **How was this a betrayal of Ish-bosheth?** This woman would have been given to Ish-bosheth like Saul's other possessions and was to ensure enough sons to continue the dynasty. Abner decided to try to produce his own heir, possibly so that he could contend for the throne. It was a challenge to the king's authority.

2 Samuel 3:8

29. How did Abner defend himself against the king's accusations? Why did he present himself as insulted instead of denying the charges? To protect himself from the truth, he became angry. Instead of denying the charges, he acted insulted over being called a prostitute for Judah. The king submitted to Abner's intimidating tactics.

2 Samuel 3:9–11

30. What was Abner's threat to Ish-bosheth, and how did Ish-bosheth respond? Abner threatened to transfer the kingdom to David instead of the house of Saul. Ish-bosheth was afraid of Abner and backed down.

2 Samuel 3:12

31. What did Abner tell David he would do? Abner sent messengers to David and told him that he would help him defeat Ish-bosheth if David promised to protect Abner's life and position.

2 Samuel 3:13

32. What was David's condition for making the treaty? David agreed to the covenant with Abner if he would bring Saul's daughter Michal back to David.

2 Samuel 3:14–15

33. What price did David have to pay before Saul would give him Michal as a wife? A hundred foreskins of the Philistines.

34. Who was Michal with when Ish-bosheth took her? She was with her new husband, Paltiel. Saul forced her to marry him after David escaped from Saul.

2 Samuel 3:16

35. What was significant about the husband's response to Michal being taken from him? How did this reflect on David's character at that time? Weeping, Paltiel followed her as far as Bahurim until Abner sent him away without her. David's cold-hearted demands hurt Michal's husband deeply. David didn't inquire of the Lord, and his actions seemed to be more political than romantic.

ANSWER KEY

Discussion Questions (Answers may vary.)

1. In Deuteronomy 17, the Lord strictly commanded that the king should not take multiple wives for himself. Other than political strategy, what could be a reason David continuously broke this law? David never stopped mourning the loss of his best and closest friend, Jonathan. He was not only a friend but an advisor. It's possible that David continuously tried to fill the loneliness in his life by seeking the company of multiple women.

2. In 2 Samuel 3, we see David's family line grow as he waited to become king over all of Israel. What are some ways the Lord made connections between David during this time and Jesus? The Lord is waiting for His people, Israel, to receive Him as King over Israel. The people rejected Jesus when He came to them the first time, and He told them that He would not return until all of Israel received Him. The Lord is bringing many sons and daughters to glory, just as David had many sons and daughters while waiting for his kingdom.

3. What were David's real intentions in asking for Michal to be returned to him? While David likely missed and still had feelings for Michal, this seems to have been more of a political move than an emotional one. David was willing to remove Michal from her current husband of seventeen years to see if Abner could deliver on his word. If Abner could make this happen, he could make other things happen for David as well. Reestablishing his marriage to Saul's daughter would also help David to appease the northern tribes by giving him, in their minds, a better claim to Saul's throne.

SESSIONS 3–4
DAVID'S OBSTACLES FALL: CHAPTERS 3:17–39; 4; & 5:1–5

CORE QUESTIONS

Background

1. What did Abner do in response to Ish-bosheth confronting him? He threw his support behind David in the south.

2. What did David do in response to Abner's proposal for a covenant between them? He asked Abner to prove himself first by sending David's first wife, Michal, to him.

2 Samuel 3:17–18

3. **Whom did Abner consult with, and what did he tell them?** The elders of Israel. He reminded them how they had previously wanted David to be king over them and told them that now they needed to act on it. Abner also told them that the Lord had spoken to David, saying that, through David, He would save Israel from the Philistines and all their enemies.

2 Samuel 3:19

4. **Who else did Abner speak with to rally the people for David? How was this ironic, given Abner's history with the people?** He spoke to the people of Benjamin. Abner's political rally here was ironic because, when Saul died, many, if not all, the tribes in the north were prepared to support David until Abner intervened. At this point, he was trying to win them back to David's side.

2 Samuel 3:20

5. **What did David do for Abner after his political campaigning? Why was this significant?** He held a feast for Abner and his men. The covenant between David and Abner would have been established with a blood sacrifice. Since an animal was killed in this process, it led to feasting as well. After everyone ate together, David sent Abner away in peace.

2 Samuel 3:21

6. **Before David sent Abner away in peace, what did Abner request from David?** That he could go and gather all of Israel so they could make a covenant with him.

2 Samuel 3:22

7. **Where was Joab while this was going on? Whom had he been fighting?** He was on a raid with his men. They had been fighting the Amalekites and brought back a considerable amount of spoil.

2 Samuel 3:23–25

8. **What did Joab tell David that Abner came to do?** He told David that Abner was lying to him and came only to spy on him and learn his ways.

Answer Key

9. **Why was Joab so upset?** After being told that Abner was there and had left in peace, Joab thought that the king had been tricked. He was also angry because Abner had killed his brother and this was a missed opportunity for revenge. Plus, David had entered into a covenant with Abner.

2 Samuel 3:26–27

10. **In his anger, what did Joab do after leaving David?** Joab sent messengers to bring Abner back from the well of Sirah without David's knowledge. Joab took Abner aside "to speak with him privately" and killed him as revenge for his brother's death.

2 Samuel 3:28

11. **What was David's first declaration after hearing of Abner's death?** He declared that, before the Lord, he and his kingdom were innocent of Abner's blood.

2 Samuel 3:29

12. **Why was David's response to Joab's crime unusual?** Normally, Joab would have been put to death. However, David spoke a curse over him and his family, that everyone in his family would come to ruin through one calamity or another. Everyone would forever know that Joab's family was cursed, and David was confident that the Lord would deal justice as it was needed.

2 Samuel 3:30

13. **Who else was involved in the conspiracy to kill Abner?** Joab's other brother, Abishai.

2 Samuel 3:31

14. **How did David show respect to Abner and declare innocence in his death?** He told everyone, including Joab, to go through the proper mourning process for Abner. He also personally walked behind the body as it was being carried.

2 Samuel 3:32–34

15. **During the funeral procession and burial, what were the main points David made in his lament?** That Abner died at the hands of criminals rather than as a war

2 Samuel

hero. That his death was not the result of a conflict between the north and the south. That it was a criminal act of violence committed by an individual.

2 Samuel 3:35

16. **Why did David refuse to eat?** David privately and publicly mourned the death of Abner. It was his way of showing grief over the man and a crime that should not have been committed.

2 Samuel 3:36–37

17. **What was the people's response to David's mourning?** The people were pleased with David's heartfelt sincerity. They understood that David was innocent of Abner's death.

2 Samuel 3:38–39

18. **As David continued to mourn and honor Abner, what did he say about the Lord? How does this reflect on David as a leader?** He said that the Lord would repay the evildoer according to his evil. David's reliance on the Lord to defend him helped in the long run, as that dependence became the source of David's strength as a leader.

2 Samuel 4:1

19. **What are three reasons Ish-bosheth lost courage after hearing of Abner's death?**

- He probably didn't know that Abner had been negotiating with David in the first place.
- He learned that David had entered into a covenant with Abner before he died.
- He learned that the elders of his tribes were ready to throw their support behind David.

2 Samuel 4:2–3

20. **Who were the two military commanders from the tribe of Benjamin? What was significant about the town they were from**? Baanah and Rechab. They lived in Beeroth, outside the territory of Benjamin. However, they were from the tribe of

Benjamin. Technically speaking, their allegiance should have been with Ish-bosheth, but they plotted against him.

2 Samuel 4:4

21. **Other than Ish-bosheth, who was the only other living relative of Saul? What made him unique?** Jonathan's son, Mephibosheth, was the only other heir to the throne. He was crippled in his feet due to an accident. His nurse fled with him when he was five after hearing of Saul and Jonathan's death, and he fell.

2 Samuel 4:5–6

22. **What was Rechab and Baanah's crime against Ish-bosheth?** In the heat of the day, when everyone was napping, they came to the house as if to get wheat, and they killed Ish-bosheth. They both escaped.

2 Samuel 4:7

23. **What did Rechab and Baanah do after killing Ish-bosheth?** They beheaded him and took his head back to Hebron by way of the Arabah.

2 Samuel 4:8

24. **Why did the men present the head of Ish-bosheth to David?** Probably expecting a reward, they proudly declared that the Lord had given David the head. They claimed that now David had vengeance on Saul for attacking him so often.

2 Samuel 4:9–11

25. **What was David's response to their presentation?** He first gave God credit for redeeming him from distress. He then reminded the men about what he did to the servant who killed Saul and stated that their blood would be required for killing Ish-bosheth in his bed.

2 Samuel 4:12

26. **How were the men killed?** David had them killed and cut off their hands and feet. He then had them hung up beside the pool in Hebron.

2 SAMUEL

27. What did David and his men do with the head of Ish-bosheth? They buried it in the grave of Abner in Hebron.

Discussion Questions (Answers may vary.)

1. David put Joab's punishment into God's hands. What are three reasons it is better to "leave room for the wrath of God," as Paul said (Romans 12:19)?

- We remain innocent of sinning through retribution of one kind or another.
- The Lord's style of punishment is always better than ours, since He has far more options at His disposal.
- The Lord can turn the situation to good in ways we cannot, perhaps even leading the person to repent and reconcile.

2. After learning of Ish-bosheth's death, David punished the men who intended to avenge him. What was David declaring by doing this? He was declaring that he didn't need rogues seeking to avenge him, because the Lord had his back. He respected the Lord's choice to allow Saul's attacks. The Lord had promised him the throne one day, so David didn't need to force it. He trusted that the Lord had a good purpose in holding the throne back from David for a time.

3. What is the historical significance of David hanging the two men's bodies by the pool in Hebron? The battle between the north and the south started at a peace negotiation around a pool (2 Samuel 2:12–32).

SESSIONS 5–6
WALKING IN THE WILL OF GOD: CHAPTERS 5 & 6:1–5

CORE QUESTIONS

2 Samuel 5:6

1. What did the people of Jebus tell David when David and his men arrived? What gave David the confidence to ignore their claims? They said that he could not enter, that the blind and lame would turn him away. However, David was led by the confidence of a man walking in the will of God.

Answer Key

2 Samuel 5:7–8

2. What was David's response to their threat? He ignored their threat and captured the stronghold of Zion.

2 Samuel 5:9–10

3. David set up his kingdom and called it the "City of David." What was the key factor in David's success? David recalled his anointing and the promises God made to his line. His success was entirely based on God being with him.

2 Samuel 5:11

4. Who built a house for David? What did he provide? Hiram, the king of Tyre, went to David with cedar trees, carpenters, and stonemasons to build his house for him.

2 Samuel 5:12

5. According to this verse, for whose sake did the Lord establish David as king over Israel? The Lord established David and exalted his kingdom for the sake of His people, Israel.

2 Samuel 5:13

6. Even though God established him as king, David still entertained what unlawful practice? David continued to take more concubines and wives. God's law allowed for one wife.

2 Samuel 5:14–16

7. What were the names of the children born to David in Jerusalem? Shammuah, Shobab, Nathan, Solomon, Ibhar, Elishua, Nepheg, Japhia, Elishama, Eliada, and Eliphelet.

2 Samuel 5:17

8. Who rose against David after he was anointed king? Why did they attack so quickly? The Philistines went up to seek out David, causing him to hide in the stronghold. They likely were hoping to defeat the new king before he had consolidated power.

2 Samuel 5:18–19

9. What was the first thing David did when faced with the enemy? He inquired of the Lord and asked if he should fight against the Philistines and if he would win.

10. What was God's reply to David, and what did He provide? The Lord said, "Go up, for I will certainly give the Philistines into your hand." He not only approved of the battle but even gave David tactical plans to ensure his victory.

2 Samuel 5:20

11. Where did David defeat the Philistines? What was the significance of the name David gave to the location? At Baal-perazim, which meant "the Lord of breaking through" or "the Lord who bursts through."

12. Whom did David credit for the victory against the Philistines? He said that the Lord broke through his enemies like the breakthrough of waters.

2 Samuel 5:21

13. What did the Philistines abandon, and what happened to them? They abandoned their idols, and David's army carried them away.

2 Samuel 5:22

14. Where did the Philistines set up camp? What was significant about this location, based on its name? They spread themselves out in the valley of Rephaim. The name meant "valley of the giants," and it was likely south of Jerusalem. (See *Encyclopedia of the Bible*, "Valley of Rephaim," https://www.biblegateway.com/resources/encyclopedia-of-the-bible/Valley-Rephaim.)

2 Samuel 5:23–24

15. When David inquired of the Lord whether he should attack, what were the Lord's instructions? He told David not to go directly up but to circle around behind the Philistines and come at them from the balsam trees. When he heard the sound of marching, then they were to act, for the Lord would have gone before them.

Answer Key

2 Samuel 5:25

16. **What was the result of the battle?** David obeyed the Lord and struck down the Philistines from Geba as far as Gezer.

2 Samuel 6:1–2

17. **Why did David gather thirty thousand chosen men of Israel? What was significant about the name of the location?** He went to Baale-judah to retrieve the ark of the Lord. The name meant "master of Judah," and it was a central location for Baal worship. (See *Strong's Concordance,* "H1184 – Baale Yehudah.")

2 Samuel 6:3

18. **What was wrong with the way David transported the ark?** God had very clear instructions for how to transport the ark. Instead of having it carried by the priests on foot, using poles with rings (Numbers 4:1–20), David put it on a new cart reserved for royal purposes.

19. **From whose house was the ark of the Lord retrieved?** The house of Abinadab.

2 Samuel 6:5

20. **David's motives were pure, although his obedience was not. In what manner did David transport the ark of the Lord?** David and all of Israel were celebrating before the Lord with instruments and dancing.

Discussion Questions (Answers may vary.)

1. **Which mountains and valleys surrounded Jerusalem?** Mount Zion, Mount Moriah, the Mount of Olives, and the Tyropoeon and Kidron valleys.

2. **How did this landscape protect the city?** The city was built between the valleys, which were very steep, making attack against the city difficult. The city was also built beside the only supply of fresh water in the region, the spring of Gihon.

3. **What did the term "blind and lame" become a euphemism for in Israel?** For the ungodly Gentiles of the land, like the Jebusites. The full saying recorded in 2 Samuel 5:8 is: "The blind or the lame shall not come into the house." "The house"

2 Samuel

was a reference to the temple of the Lord in Jerusalem, so this was a way of saying that ungodly Gentiles could not enter the temple.

4. **Whom was David comparable to, regarding his large family of multiple wives and his children by them?** Facts like this are descriptive, not prescriptive. In other words, they tell us what happened, not what God wants us to do. David was comparable to Jacob, who had four wives and twelve sons. While God did not bless the actions, he still blessed their family as a result of His promise to them. We could never obey enough to earn God's blessing, so He often blesses despite our shortcomings.

5. **Who are the two children of David mentioned in Jesus' genealogy, and what makes them significant?** Solomon and Nathan are both mentioned in Jesus' genealogy (Matthew 1:1–17 and Luke 3:23–38, respectively). Mary descended from Nathan, and Joseph descended from Solomon.

6. **How did Saul go against God's wishes regarding the ark of the Lord?** Saul took the ark of the Lord in Shiloh into battle to ensure his success. Saul tried to force God's hand, so the Lord allowed the ark to be taken by the Philistines (1 Samuel 4:1–11).

Session 7A
True Worship Is Obedience: Chapters 6:6–23 & 7:1–16

Background

2 Samuel 6:1–5

1. **From where did David and his men retrieve the ark of the Lord?** They retrieved the ark from Baale-judah.

2. **How did the Lord instruct the people to move the ark of the Lord?** The priests were the only ones allowed to handle the ark. They had to carry it on long poles with rings on them, and the men had to be on foot (Numbers 4:1–20).

3. **Whom did David gather to go with him to retrieve the ark of the Lord, and how many were there?** Thirty thousand chosen men of Israel.

4. **Who was leading the new cart carrying the ark of the Lord?** Uzzah and Ahio, the sons of Abinadab. (The ark was at Abinadab's house before David retrieved it.)

ANSWER KEY

CORE QUESTIONS

2 Samuel 6:6

5. What did Uzzah do to the ark of the Lord? He reached out and took hold of it. The oxen nearly made it fall, and he was trying to stop it from falling.

2 Samuel 6:7

6. Why was God angry with Uzzah? Even though Uzzah was trying to steady the ark, God's word in Numbers 4 said that if a non-priest touched the ark, he would die. God always keeps His word.

7. How was Uzzah being irreverent by trying to protect the ark? This word is better translated "error" (KJV), referring to the error in judgment rather than Uzzah's act. The problem was David's mistake in ordering Uzzah and the other men to transport the ark improperly.

2 Samuel 6:8–9

8. David became angry with the Lord for striking Uzzah as a punishment. What emotion did David have, along with anger, that affected his next decision? He was afraid of the Lord and the ark.

2 Samuel 6:10–11

9. What did David decide to do after the Lord's punishment, and what was the result of David refusing to bring the ark into Jerusalem? David changed his plans. Instead of bringing the ark to Jerusalem, he took it to the house of Obed-edom the Gittite for three months. The man's entire household was blessed because of it.

2 Samuel 6:12

10. What changed David's mind about reinstating the plan to bring the ark into Jerusalem? David found out that the house of Obed-edom was being blessed on account of the ark.

2 Samuel 6:13

11. **What did David do in repentance as they brought the ark back to the tabernacle?** David sacrificed an ox and a fatling every six paces they walked.

2 Samuel 6:14–15

12. **How were David and the people celebrating on the way back to Jerusalem?** They were dancing, shouting, and sounding the trumpet.

13. **What was David wearing, and why?** David was wearing a linen ephod, the sleeveless white robe the priests wore. He likely wanted to identify himself as one of them to show that he would take the fall if God acted against them this time around.

2 Samuel 6:16

14. **Why did Michal despise David when she saw him return with the ark?** David had ripped Michal away from the husband she loved, so she was probably already bitter toward him. She might have been jealous of David's relationship with the Lord but was likely also embarrassed by his undignified display.

2 Samuel 6:17–18

15. **What was the first thing David did after bringing the ark into the prepared tent?** David offered burnt offerings and peace offerings before the Lord. Then he blessed the people in the name of the Lord.

2 Samuel 6:19

16. **Which gifts from his storehouse did David give to the people?** He gave each person a cake of bread, a cake of dates, and a cake of raisins.

17. **What did the gifts represent?** These treats commonly represented prosperity and fertility. (See *Encyclopedia of the Bible,* "Raisin-Cakes," https://www.biblegateway.com/resources/encyclopedia-of-the-bible/Raisin-Cakes.)

2 Samuel 6:20

18. **What was Michal's primary complaint to David?** Highly sarcastic, she complained that he was parading about shamelessly, uncovered and undignified.

2 Samuel 6:21–22

19. **How did David correct his wife, and whom did he credit for his kingship?** David told her that the Lord appointed him ruler over Israel instead of her father. He gave the Lord full credit for giving him the throne and said that was why he would always celebrate before the Lord.

20. **What character trait did David show in his response to her?** He demonstrated humility before God and in his own eyes, yet he knew that God would distinguish him before the people of Israel.

2 Samuel 6:21–23

21. **What was significant about the fact that Michal never had a child?** Michal was Saul's daughter. If she had a son, then the boy would have been able to contend for the throne of David due to being in Saul's bloodline. However, God ended that line when Saul died.

2 Samuel 7:1–3

22. **David had rest from all his enemies, but he was bothered that the ark of God was in a meager tent. What did the prophet Nathan tell him?** He told David to go do everything he wanted to do because the Lord was with him.

2 Samuel 7:4–7

23. **What did the Lord tell Nathan the prophet in response to his initial words to David?** The Lord told him to go to David and remind him that He had not dwelt in a house since the day He brought up the sons of Israel from Egypt. God didn't need a house of cedar, and He never asked for one.

2 Samuel 7:8

24. **How did God gently remind David of his place?** He reminded David that he was a shepherd, following sheep, and the Lord placed him as ruler over the people.

2 Samuel 7:9–11

25. What did the Lord promise David? That He would make his name great, that He would plant His people in a permanent place, and that He would give David rest from his enemies. Finally, he promised to make a house for David.

2 Samuel 7:12–13

26. What did the Lord tell David would happen after he died? That his son would rule after him, and he would build God's house.

2 Samuel 7:14–16

27. What did God promise would happen when his son would inevitably fall into sin? That God would correct him with human consequences. However, He would not remove him from the throne as He did with Saul.

28. What is the set of promises the Lord made to David called? The Davidic Covenant.

Discussion Questions (Answers may vary.)

1. **If God had not acted against Uzzah, then He would have been violating His word in Numbers 4. What would have happened if God had made an exception for Uzzah and not kept His word?** If God could violate His word whenever it suited Him, then we would have no reason to trust in any of His promises.

2. **David became angry and fearful of God when He killed Uzzah. Why do we often feel that way toward God when we endure His discipline?** Often we lash out, believing that we are being treated unfairly. We may think that God is being unpredictable and neglectful. However, our disobedience, not God, is to blame.

3. **Why does the Bible place such high demands of character and knowledge on anyone who would lead God's people?** A godly leader will bear the fruit of knowledgeable and obedient followers of Jesus. An unqualified and untrustworthy leader will yield ignorant and disobedient followers.

4. **David immediately recognized that Michal's true concerns were not with his dignity as king. What was her outburst about?** She was upset about her relationship with David and David's relationship with the Lord.

Answer Key

Session 7B
Awaiting a Promised Kingdom: Chapter 7

Background

2 Samuel 7:4–16

1. **What was the likely reason David proposed to build God a temple in place of the tent?** David was probably self-conscious that his house was large and impressive and the Lord's was only a tent. However, good intentions are not an excuse for disobedience.

2. **To interpret the covenants of God, including the Davidic Covenant, properly, the law of suggested fulfillment can be used. How does this explain the delayed fulfillment?** Things may appear to fulfill a promise of God but fall short in some way. Events may hint at or suggest the eventual fulfillment of a covenant, but they are not the actual fulfillment.

3. **In the Abrahamic and Davidic Covenants, who is the future King that God was referencing, and which kingdom will He bring?** The future King is Jesus, the Messiah, and He will bring about the Millennial Kingdom.

4. **Which new details did the Lord give in the Davidic Covenant that were never given to Abraham?** A descendent of David will build a house for God, and his throne will be established forever. Because of sins committed, God will chasten him, but He promised never to take away His lovingkindness from him. His throne will last forever.

Core Questions

2 Samuel 7:17–18

5. **What was the first thing David did when the prophet Nathan told him not to build a house for God?** David went in and sat before the Lord in humility, acknowledging His grace and provision.

2 Samuel 7:19–21

6. **What was David in awe of as he was praying?** He was overwhelmed that God would disclose future plans to him, ones that would honor his lineage and make him a

2 Samuel

part of a greater plan. David said that the wonderful things God had done for him were insignificant compared to His revelation.

2 Samuel 7:22–24

7. **For whom did God redeem Israel, and why?** David acknowledged in his prayer that God redeemed Israel for Himself and to make a name for Himself.

2 Samuel 7:25

8. **What did David pray the Lord would do after he received this word from Him?** David asked the Lord to confirm it forever and to do as He said. David was aligning himself with the plans of God and essentially saying, "Amen," to everything God had promised.

2 Samuel 7:26–27

9. **What gave David the courage to pray?** God choosing to honor him with a revelation of the future gave him the courage.

2 Samuel 7:28–29

10. **What did David request of God?** He asked that the house of David would continue forever before the Lord and be blessed forever.

Discussion Questions (Answers may vary.)

1. **In verse 7, the Lord reminded David that God never commanded Israel to build His house in any form other than a tent. What is good advice to follow when deciding whether to take on another task for the Lord?** When you wonder what you should do to obey God, always do the last thing He told you. Keep doing that until you hear the Lord clearly tell you to do something else.

2. **What were the three errors David made in assuming that he could build God a house for the ark of the Lord?**

- He ignored history.
- He acted without God's direction.
- He presumed too much for himself.

ANSWER KEY

3. **In what two ways did the fulfillment of prophetic events from the days of Joshua up to David not fulfill the Abrahamic Covenant?** The people of Israel could not hold the land, yet the promise to Abraham was that Israel would have it forever. Israel was constantly fighting enemies and losing ground, but the promise was to live in peace.

4. **When Jesus returns, how long does Revelation 20 say His kingdom will last?** One thousand years.

5. **What are two ways we know that David's son Solomon was not the fulfillment of the coming king the Lord referenced in His revelation?** In 2 Samuel 7:12, God said that He would raise up a descendant after David died, but David moved to have Solomon anointed king before David died (1 Kings 1). The covenant also revealed that Solomon's throne would go on forever, but it didn't last even one generation after he died, being split into two kingdoms instead (1 Kings 11–12; 2 Chronicles 10–12).

SESSIONS 8–9
A GOD WHO KEEPS LOVINGKINDNESS: CHAPTERS 8 & 9

Background

1. **What blessings did David experience as a result of God's anointing?** David's blessings came in the form of his growing family and wealth and the nation's military, economic, and religious strength.

2. **What did the Lord promise David through His covenant with him?** God promised to preserve David's dynasty forever through a ruler to come. Under that ruler, there would come an eternal Kingdom that would fulfill the promises God gave to Israel.

CORE QUESTIONS

2 Samuel 8:1

3. **What was significant about the city that David overthrew?** It was the chief city of the Philistines.

2 Samuel 8:2

4. **How did David divide the defeated Moabites, and for what purpose?** David made the Moabites lie on the ground, and he measured two lines of them. The first was put to death, and the second group became his servants.

2 Samuel 8:3–4

5. **When David defeated Hadadezer—the son of Rehob, king of Zobah—what did he do with the chariot horses he captured? Why would he do this?** He "hamstrung" the horses, meaning that he cut the tendons in their legs, rendering them useless as animals for war.

2 Samuel 8:5–6

6. **What did David do with the Arameans when they arrived to help Hadadezer?** He forced them to become his servants.

2 Samuel 8:7–10

7. **What precious metals did David take back to Jerusalem from his conquests?** He took shields of gold and a very large amount of bronze. He also received articles of silver, gold, and bronze as gifts from Hamath.

2 Samuel 8:11–12

8. **What did David do with the precious spoils of the nations he subdued?** He dedicated them to the Lord.

2 Samuel 8:13–14

9. **David's military victories brought extensive wealth to Israel and boosted his reputation. To what did the writer attribute David's victories?** He said that the Lord helped David wherever he went.

2 Samuel 8:15

10. **What was David known for during his reign over Israel?** He administered justice and righteousness for all his people.

ANSWER KEY

2 Samuel 8:16–18

11. What position did Joab hold in David's kingdom? What positions did David's sons hold? Joab was over the army. David's sons were chief ministers at the king's side.

2 Samuel 9:1

12. Why did David want to show kindness to a living family member of Saul? David remembered the covenant he entered into with Jonathan.

2 Samuel 9:2–3

13. Who did Ziba, the servant of the house, tell David was still living? Jonathan's son, who was crippled in both feet.

2 Samuel 9:4–5

14. What did David do when he heard of Jonathan's son? He sent and brought him from the house of Machir, the son of Ammiel, from Lo-debar.

2 Samuel 9:6

15. What was Mephibosheth's reaction to being summoned to David? Likely afraid for his life, Jonathan's son fell on his face and prostrated himself before David, calling himself David's servant.

2 Samuel 9:7

16. What three things did David tell Mephibosheth he would do for him?

- David would show kindness to him for the sake of Jonathan, his father.
- He would restore all Saul's land to him.
- Mephibosheth would eat regularly at David's table.

2 Samuel 9:8

17. Why did Mephibosheth call himself a dead dog? The dog was the worst creature in Jewish eyes, so it would be the worst insult you could call someone. The only thing

2 SAMUEL

lower than a dog was a dead dog. Mephibosheth knew that as a crippled man, he had no worth to David, and even more, David could see him as an enemy.

2 Samuel 9:9–10

18. **What command did David give to the servant Ziba? What are the likely reasons David assigned this lesser post to him?** He commanded Ziba, his sons, and his servants to cultivate the land for Mephibosheth and to harvest the produce as food for him. He also let Ziba know that Mephibosheth would eat regularly at the king's table. David likely assigned Ziba this post since he had fifteen sons and twenty servants, which meant that he had a lot of labor at his disposal. He also might have wanted an ally close to Mephibosheth.

2 Samuel 9:11

19. **Who else ate with the king at his table?** The king's sons ate with David at his table, so Mephibosheth became as one of his sons.

Discussion Questions (Answers may vary.)

1. **Why did David have the men of Moab lie on the ground?** David measured the height of the men according to a "line." Ones who measured one line were allowed to live (likely the young men). The ones who measured to the second line were killed. Even in his conquest, David showed mercy by allowing some men to live. This might have been due to his grandmother, Ruth, being a Moabite.

2. **What was the significance of David having many defeated enemies become servants instead of wiping them out?** Besides showing mercy, the Lord was producing a picture of Jesus through David. When His kingdom arrives on the earth, the enemies that surround Israel will become her servants.

3. **What were the details of David's covenant with Jonathan?** Jonathan promised to help David stay alive despite his father's attempt to kill him. Jonathan agreed to become a spy for David and rebel against the king. In exchange, Jonathan asked David to preserve his life once David assumed power. He also asked that David not cut off anyone in Saul's household.

4. **What was the significance of Mephibosheth being invited to eat regularly at the king's table?** To eat with another person held great significance in that culture.

It was a place of fellowship, privilege, and implied protection. Covenants were usually established with meals. Eating at the king's table implied friendship with the king.

SESSIONS 10–11
A CORRUPTED HEART: CHAPTERS 10 & 11

Background

1. **In chapter 9, we see Mephibosheth crippled and on his face before King David. How is this an image of us as human beings?** Just as Mephibosheth became disabled by a fall, so are we disabled spiritually by a fall into sin. Just as he couldn't stand in David's presence, neither can we stand in the presence of God by our efforts.

2. **How did David's response to Mephibosheth present a picture of Jesus?** When David looked at Mephibosheth, he saw his friend Jonathan. When the Father looks upon us, He sees Jesus. God shows us mercy because of a covenant made in Jesus' blood, just like the mercy David showed in response to a covenant he made with Jonathan.

3. **What did David give Mephibosheth that would set the stage for future conflict?** He gave Mephibosheth his grandfather's inheritance of land in the tribe of Benjamin.

CORE QUESTIONS

2 Samuel 10:1–2

4. **What did David do for the new king of the Ammonites when his father died?** To show kindness to Hanun, he sent some of his servants to console him concerning his father.

2 Samuel 10:3

5. **What did the Ammonite princes tell the king that David was actually doing?** They said that David sent his servants to search the city, to spy it out, and overthrow it.

2 Samuel 10:4

6. **What did King Hanun do to David's servants?** Shaved off half of their beards, cut off their garments, and sent them away.

7. **What made these actions so insulting to David's men?** Jews didn't shave their beards or heads, because the law prohibited it (Leviticus 19:27). This was a deliberate humiliation to the people. Sending them away barely clothed added to their embarrassment.

2 Samuel 10:5

8. **How did David sensitively reassure his men when they were humiliated?** He told them to stay at Jericho until their beards grew back. This would naturally take several months, but Jericho was the perfect hiding place for them since it had never been rebuilt since Joshua's day.

2 Samuel 10:6

9. **What were the Ammonites expecting when they hired military help from their allies?** They were preparing for the inevitable war their king invited by his actions toward David's men.

2 Samuel 10:7–8

10. **When David heard that the Ammonites and Arameans were gathering for war, he sent Joab and his army to the front. What was different about this response versus the other battles David had fought?** David did not consult the Lord before going to war, as he once did. Also, David wasn't fighting in this battle as he had before.

2 Samuel 10:9–11

11. **Joab divided the troops and set his brother, Abishai, over the second half. Who were the two enemy groups they were set against? Why did he assign the second troop to his brother?** Joab was set against the Arameans, and his brother, Abishai, was set against the sons of Ammon. Joab knew that he would have to fight on two fronts simultaneously, so he divided his forces for higher chances of victory and so one troop could support the other if it faltered.

2 Samuel 10:12

12. **What was Joab's rally cry to his fighting men?** He told them to be strong and courageous for the sake of the people and the cities of God. He said for the Lord to do what was good in His sight.

ANSWER KEY

2 Samuel 10:13–14

13. **What was the outcome of the battle?** The Lord brought Israel victory.

14. **Joab returned to Jerusalem without pursuing the fleeing enemy. What did this mean for the future?** It meant that the battle wasn't over.

2 Samuel 10:15–16

15. **What did King Hadadezer of Zobah do to strengthen his rivalry with David?** He offered his commander and army to join with the Arameans against David.

2 Samuel 10:17–18

16. **David went to war with the Arameans and was victorious. Which significant character did he kill in the battle?** He struck down and killed Shobach, the commander of their army.

2 Samuel 10:19

17. **What did the servants of Hadadezer do after David defeated them?** They made peace with Israel and served them.

2 Samuel 11:1

18. **What did David do in the spring that would have been considered wrong for kings to do?** He sent Joab and his armies to fight the sons of Ammon, but he stayed behind in Jerusalem.

19. **What did this action suggest about David's leadership at this point?** It suggested that David was delegating his God-given role as leader of Israel in battle, which meant abdicating his responsibility.

2 Samuel 11:2

20. **What was the likely reason David was walking on his rooftop in the evening?** David was likely having trouble sleeping due to the heat. Daytime heat was absorbed by the clay and stone walls, so families cooled off on the roof at night.

2 SAMUEL

21. Based on the location of Bathsheba's home, what does her bathing on the rooftop at that time of day imply? That while she might not have been seeking to sleep with David, she might have been toying with him, knowing that there was a good chance he would see her.

2 Samuel 11:3–4

22. What does James 1:14–15 say about the spiral into sin? It says that we are tempted when we are enticed and carried away by our own lust. Lust then gives birth to sin, and sin brings death.

2 Samuel 11:5

23. What was the immediate result of their adultery? What did the law require for their sin, based on Leviticus 20:10? Bathsheba became pregnant. The law demanded death for both David and Bathsheba, which was likely why she came to him and told him about the baby.

2 Samuel 11:6–7

24. Rather than confessing and seeking Uriah's forgiveness, what did David inquire about when he summoned Uriah from the battlefront? He asked about the state of the war, as if he were only checking on the status of the battle.

2 Samuel 11:8–9

25. In what way did Uriah honorably disobey the king? David told him to go to his house and enjoy his night. He even sent gifts of extra food and rations for him to celebrate at home. Uriah, however, was a man of honor and integrity, and he chose to sleep in the house of David's servants.

26. What was David's purpose behind this, and how did Uriah's actions frustrate his plans? David expected Uriah to go home and sleep with his wife, hoping that would be seen as the cause of his wife's pregnancy. When Uriah refused to go, it would be clear that the pregnancy was the result of adultery.

2 Samuel 11:10–11

27. When David asked him why he refused to go to his home, what was Uriah's response? Uriah answered that he couldn't bring himself to enjoy the things others

ANSWER KEY

couldn't do under the circumstances. He said that if the ark wasn't in a proper home and his commander and comrades were living in a field, then he couldn't stay in his home and lie with his wife.

2 Samuel 11:12

28. **What was David's next command to Uriah?** To stay the night again, and tomorrow he would send him back to the battlefront.

2 Samuel 11:13

29. **After the first attempt failed, what was David's second attempt to have Uriah sleep with his wife?** He got Uriah drunk, expecting him to sleep with his wife that evening. However, he would not go to his house.

2 Samuel 11:14–15

30. **What was David's command to Joab as his final attempt to hide his adultery?** To place Uriah in the front line of the fiercest battle and then withdraw from him so he would be killed.

2 Samuel 11:16–17

31. **David's command was obeyed, and all went according to plan. However, who else suffered from this decision?** More of David's men died as a result of their battle plan. Their blood and Uriah's was on David's head.

2 Samuel 11:18–21

32. **What was the purpose of delaying the news of Uriah's death until after David was upset about the battle plan that was executed?** If Joab had sent a messenger to tell David that Uriah was dead, it would have been obvious that David had ordered it. By causing David to get angry at his commander's foolish plan of attack, he could sneak in the news. This would calm David's anger and make the announcement of Uriah's death seem natural and unassociated from David.

2 Samuel 11:22–25

33. What was David's response to Joab regarding Uriah's death? He told him not to see what was done as evil. David did this to soften his guilt and Joab's. He also encouraged him to strengthen his battle and overthrow the city.

2 Samuel 11:26–27

34. When Bathsheba's mourning period for her husband was over, what did David do? David brought her to his house to become his wife, and she bore him a son.

35. What was the divine judgment on David's actions? What David had done was evil in God's sight.

Discussion Questions (Answers may vary.)

1. What could David have done when he first saw Bathsheba bathing instead of allowing his lust to lead him to adultery and murder? David should have averted his eyes to stop lust from carrying him away. He could have sent messengers to order Bathsheba to bathe inside from then on.

2. What was interesting about Bathsheba bathing *after* she and David engaged in adultery? She was concerned about keeping the law's requirements for ritual cleansing but was willing to violate the law's demand for purity. She used one against the other. She committed adultery but then used ritual cleansing to try to offset the sin.

3. Based on Genesis 3:6, what is a person's instinctive response after engaging in sin? We expect others to join us in that sin and even encourage them to do so. Such was the case with David bringing Joab into his murderous plot against Uriah.

ANSWER KEY

SESSION 12
SIN EXPOSED: CHAPTER 12

CORE QUESTIONS

2 Samuel 12:1–4

1. **Whom did God enlist to confront David about his sin?** The prophet Nathan.

2. **Whom did the flocks and ewe lamb represent in Nathan's parable?** The flocks and herds were David's many wives and concubines. The one little ewe lamb was Uriah's one wife, Bathsheba.

2 Samuel 12:5–6

3. **What was David's natural response upon hearing of the rich man who took and killed the ewe lamb?** David was angry at the rich man and said that he deserved to die. He demanded that restitution be made fourfold. Unknowingly, he was announcing his own sentence, which was Nathan's intent.

2 Samuel 12:7–8

4. **When Nathan pronounced David guilty, what did he remind David that the Lord had done and would do?** That the Lord anointed him king over Israel and delivered him from Saul. That He gave David Saul's house and wives, as well as all of Israel and Judah. If David had asked, He would have added even more than this to him.

2 Samuel 12:9–12

5. **After revealing that David's sin was known, what four things did the Lord pronounce in judgment over the house of David?** That the sword would never depart from his house, that He would raise up evil against him from his household, that He would take David's wives and give them to his companion, and that He would do everything before all of Israel.

2 Samuel 12:13

6. **What was David's first response to Nathan's pronouncement?** He embraced humility and repentance, admitting that he had sinned against the Lord.

2 Samuel

7. Even after revealing everything, what amazing statement did Nathan make after David confessed? He said that the Lord had taken away his sin, and he would not die because of it.

2 Samuel 12:14

8. Although he was forgiven, restitution still had to be made for David's murder of Uriah. What was the consequence of that sin? What did it cause among Israel's enemies? It gave Israel's enemies license to blaspheme the Lord, as they saw Him as no different from their pagan gods.

2 Samuel 12:15

9. What was the first punishment the Lord brought to pass? The death of David and Bathsheba's son. The Lord struck the child so that he was very sick.

2 Samuel 12:16–17

10. What was David's response when his son became sick? He fasted and prostrated himself in prayer.

2 Samuel 12:18–19

11. Why were David's servants whispering, and what were they afraid of when the boy died? While the child was alive, David would not listen to the servants; he stayed in fasting and prayer. They were trying to avoid telling him that his child had died because they were afraid that he would harm himself in his grief.

2 Samuel 12:20

12. When David heard of his son's death, what was his first response? He arose from the ground, washed, anointed himself, and changed clothes. Then he went into the house of the Lord to worship. After he worshipped, he went home and ate.

2 Samuel 12:21

13. Why were the servants confused by David's behavior? In Jewish culture, mourning for a death was an elaborate and ritualized process. David did none of those things.

2 Samuel 12:22–23

14. **What was David's explanation for his behavior?** He said that he was fasting and praying for the child to live, hoping the Lord would be gracious to him. Since God had already pronounced His judgment before the boy died, once he did, there wasn't anything that would bring him back.

Discussion Questions (Answers may vary.)

1. **How would events have played out differently if David had been devoted to his first and only wife, Michal?** If David had been a one-wife king as was commanded, he would not have seen every woman as a potential conquest. As his lust turned into multiple marriages, this gave him supposed grounds to murder to obtain his next object of lust.

2. **God called David's sin despising the word of the Lord (2 Samuel 12:9). How did David sin against the word of the Lord?** When we go against God's commands, we show contempt for Him and His word. We take for granted the grace we are given through the revelation of that word and the other blessings we receive.

3. **In verse 10, Nathan said that the sword would never depart from David's house. What was the meaning of this euphemism? In what three specific ways would it come about?** It meant that David's house would not know peace. His house would suffer three penalties, one for each of the ten commandments David broke:

- For coveting, members of David's household would covet his wives.
- For adultery, some in David's household would lie with his wives, committing adultery with them.
- For murder, David's child would die.

4. **About what did Nathan reassure David regarding David's sins?** That his sins did not separate him from God because the Lord had taken David's sins away.

5. **What are the four main reasons the Lord disciplines His children?**

- To remove sin from our lives
- To turn a bad situation into a good testimony

2 Samuel

- To show the world that our sin was not approved or desired
- To remind God's children that sin displeases Him so that our lives can be a testimony one way or another

SESSION 13
THE CONSEQUENCES OF DAVID'S SIN: CHAPTER 13:1–22

Background

1. **Why was it necessary for the Lord to expose and discipline David regarding his sin?** The Lord needed to protect His name among the nations. The world needed to see that David's sin brought severe consequences so no one could claim that God approved. The nation of Israel was to be a light to the world as a representative of God's righteous ways.

2. **According to Psalm 51:3–4, what did David recognize in the death of his son?** He recognized his part in his son's death and the Lord's right to discipline him in the way He chose.

3. **After these events, David and Bathsheba conceived again. What two names were given to the boy, and what did they mean?** The boy was named Solomon from the Hebrew word *shalom*, meaning fullness, completeness, or peace. The prophet Nathan gave him the pet name Jedidiah—that is, "beloved of Yahweh"— for the Lord's sake. (See *Easton's Bible Dictionary*, "Jedidiah.")

4. **What was God's promise in the Davidic Covenant?** That a descendant of David, Jesus, would reign in a day to come.

5. **What do the terms *loved* and *hated* by God mean in reference to Solomon and Jacob?** To be loved by God meant to be chosen and set apart by God. To be hated meant that an individual was not chosen by God.

6. **The Lord continued to bless David in warfare. Which people group did he defeat in 2 Samuel 12:26–31?** He defeated the Ammonites, returning to Jerusalem with countless spoils.

Answer Key

Core Questions

2 Samuel 13:1–2

7. **Who was Tamar, and who inappropriately longed for her?** She was the daughter of David by Maacah and the half-sister of Amnon, who lusted after her.

2 Samuel 13:3

8. **Who was the shrewd man who was friends with Amnon?** Jonadab was Amnon's cousin, the son of David's brother, Shimeah.

2 Samuel 13:4

9. **What was Amnon's complaint to Jonadab?** That he was depressed to the point of making himself ill, longing for Tamar.

2 Samuel 13:5

10. **What was Jonadab's advice to Amnon?** Jonadab suggested that Ammon pretend to be ill and request Tamar to come cook for and feed him.

11. **Why did Jonadab want to help Amnon? How were his motives selfish?** He wanted to gain a friend in David's successor. He saw an opportunity to pit one brother against another and, either way, to gain favor through his friendships.

2 Samuel 13:6

12. **Who was the first person Amnon manipulated when enacting Jonadab's plan?** The first person he manipulated was the king, his father.

2 Samuel 13:7–8

13. **Without hesitation, David ordered Tamar to prepare food for Amnon. Why did it matter if she made food in his sight?** Through the doorway, he could watch her work. Again, this allowed the lust of the eyes to drive him toward sin.

2 Samuel 13:9

14. **What did Amnon refuse to do when Tamar prepared the food for him?** He refused to eat from the pan and told everyone else to leave the room.

2 Samuel 13:10–11

15. **What did Amnon command Tamar to do?** First, he told her to bring the food into his bedroom so he could eat from her hand. When she did, he then demanded that she sleep with him.

2 Samuel 13:12–13

16. **What were Tamar's arguments against sleeping with her brother?** That it would be a violation, that such a thing was disgraceful and not to be done in Israel. She argued that she would never be rid of the act against her (likely never be able to marry) and that Amnon would be seen as a fool. She even offered for him to ask David to marry her so at least she'd be taken care of.

2 Samuel 13:14

17. **What was the result of Amnon's lust and Tamar's pleading?** He overpowered and raped her.

2 Samuel 13:15

18. **After the act, what did Amnon feel toward Tamar?** He hated her with more passion than he had previously desired her. He demanded that she get away from him.

2 Samuel 13:16–17

19. **Why would sending her away add to the evil of his action?** Though the law prohibited marriage between them, she was hopeful that some solution might be found. The one thing she didn't want was to be rejected by the only man who could marry her with her honor intact.

ANSWER KEY

2 Samuel 13:18–19

20. **What was Tamar's response to being thrown out of her brother's room?** She tore the long-sleeved garment, which signified her virginity, and put ashes on her head in mourning. She held her head, crying aloud as she went away.

2 Samuel 13:20

21. **Why did Absalom tell Tamar to remain silent about the rape, and what kindness did Absalom show Tamar?** He promised to take care of her in his home as a spinster forever since she would probably never be married. He was also working out a plan for future revenge and an attempt at the throne.

Discussion Questions (Answers may vary.)

1. **Normally, the king's oldest son would be expected to inherit the throne, but Solomon was destined to rule after David. What was his placement in the succession?** Solomon was the seventh-born son of David.

2. **How did the birth of Solomon show God's blessing over His children, even when they sin?** David and Bathsheba's first son died as a result of David's sin. This child was conceived in infidelity and, as such, would not have been in line for the throne. After they were married, they had Solomon, and he was chosen by God as David's successor. Their first son was replaced by a promised one. God turns all circumstances to good.

3. **How did David's victory over the Ammonites sit as a bookend in the story of his sin?** The Lord was working through David to defeat the Ammonites, but his sin with Bathsheba and against Uriah paused that progress. God led David through the battle with his flesh and disciplined him until he repented. At that point, God picked David back up where he left off, and he defeated his longtime enemy.

4. **How was what happened between Amnon and Tamar a consequence of David's sin of taking multiple wives?** It created unnatural desires and jealousies. It also made a way for Amnon to develop a perverted view of women as objects of lust.

5. **How would Jonadab's shrewdness help him in a battle between Amnon and Absalom?** If Amnon became king, then he would remember Jonadab's helpful counsel. By encouraging Amnon to take Tamar, he also set up Absalom to take

2 Samuel

revenge and eliminate a rival. Either way, he could play the situation to his advantage to gain the favor of the winner.

6. **According to the law, what should have happened to Amnon after he raped Tamar?** He was to be cut off from the nation, which may have meant being put to death. In the interest of righteousness and in defense of his daughter, David should have sought justice for Amnon's crime.

SESSION 14
SYSTEMIC ISSUES IN DAVID'S FAMILY: CHAPTER 14

Background

1. **Why would it have been natural for Absalom to invite the king and his family to shear the sheep in Baal-hazor (2 Samuel 13:23)?** Sheep shearing happened a few times a year, and there was great feasting at night after a hard day's work. It was normal for family members to join in the festivities, and Absalom had a herd in Baal-hazor.

2. **In 2 Samuel 13:25–27, David turned down the invitation but agreed for Amnon and the other brothers to attend. Why would David have agreed, knowing the history of hatred between Absalom and Amnon?** It had been two years since Amnon's crime, and Absalom had instructed Tamar to keep quiet about the incident. The drama had likely died down, and David felt obligated to allow his sons to attend the festivities after he turned down the invitation.

3. **How did Absalom plan to kill Amnon in 2 Samuel 13:28–29?** When Amnon was drunk, the servants were to rise and kill him. He told them not to fear, because he was the one who ordered it. His servants did, and the other brothers fled the scene of the crime.

4. **According to verses 30–31, what rumors spread to David before his sons had time to return to the palace?** That Absalom had killed all of David's sons. David tore his clothes in grief and lay on the ground. His servants mourned as well.

5. **What was Jonadab's part in the murder, and how was he able to reassure the king?** Jonadab was not at the shearing party, so we can only assume that he knew about the events due to conspiracy with Absalom.

6. **In 2 Samuel 13:34–36, we see David's sons returning home. How did Jonadab deliver this news to the king?** He said, "…according to your servant's word, so it

Answer Key

happened." He was attempting to solidify the fact that he had reassured the king with this outcome, and that's what happened.

7. How long was Absalom in exile after killing his brother Amnon, and where did he go? He fled to Geshur in Upper Galilee and spent three years in exile (2 Samuel 13:38).

Core Questions

2 Samuel 14:1–3

8. What was Joab's purpose in having a woman pretend to be a mourner? He knew how much David longed for Absalom, and he wanted their relationship restored. Joab and everyone else believed that the next in line would be Absalom, and Joab didn't want him to remain in hiding.

2 Samuel 14:4–6

9. What lie did the woman tell David to set up a parallel story? She told him that she was a widow and one of her sons killed the other.

2 Samuel 14:7

10. What was she asking for in light of her story? She asked that the son who had committed murder would be pardoned so that she would not be without an heir or anyone to take care of her.

2 Samuel 14:8–10

11. What was David's response to the woman? He told her to go home and that he would send orders to her later.

2 Samuel 14:11

12. To get an immediate decision, she pressed David, saying that she feared for her and her son's lives due to the people who wanted justice. What did she convince David to do? David gave in and said that not one hair of her son would fall to the ground.

2 Samuel 14:12–17

13. What was the primary argument the woman made for David to pardon Absalom? If it was acceptable for the king to pardon some obscure mother's son, why not the heir to the throne?

14. What biblical truth did the woman point out in an unbiblical fashion? She said that our lives are short and that God is not in the business of taking life but saving it. Therefore, the quest of life should be to find God's plan for how banished ones can be restored to Him. It's a misuse to demand justice against God's laws. Mercy doesn't mean that there shouldn't be accountability.

2 Samuel 14:18–20

15. David suspected that the woman was lying, so he asked her if Joab was behind her story. What was her answer? She admitted that Joab had commanded her to speak those words to change the appearance of the king's situation.

2 Samuel 14:21

16. What did David tell Joab in response to the woman's story? He told Joab to go and bring Absalom back.

2 Samuel 14:22–23

17. How did Joab react to the king? Whom did he retrieve after their conversation? He fell on his face and blessed the king, essentially thanking him for pardoning Absalom. He then left to retrieve Absalom from Geshur.

2 Samuel 14:24

18. What was David's requirement upon Absalom's return? That Absalom go to his house and not see David.

2 Samuel 14:25–27

19. What physical attributes was Absalom known for? He was regarded as the most handsome by public opinion. He had long, thick hair and made an annual show of cutting it.

ANSWER KEY

20. **Who were Absalom's children?** He had three sons and one daughter, Tamar.

2 Samuel 14:28

21. **How long was Absalom in Jerusalem without seeing the king?** Two years.

Discussion Questions (Answers may vary.)

1. **How did Jonadab attempt a third angle with David at the news of Amnon's death?** He played the role of comforter and wise counselor. He spoke as if he were only making an educated guess as to the outcome of the rumors. In the end, he knew that David would appreciate his apparent wisdom and be pleased with him.

2. **In addition to God's discipline of taking the life of David's child, what were six other family consequences of David's poor choices up to this point?**

- David developed an attitude of favoritism toward his children and turned a blind eye to Amnon's sins.
- This dismissal allowed Amnon to lust after and rape Tamar.
- Amnon's crimes led Absalom to hate his brother, leading to division within the family.
- This forced David to protect Amnon by keeping the brothers apart.
- The separation and lack of justice furthered Absalom's resentment, leading him to act in revenge by killing Amnon.
- This resulted in Absalom fleeing into exile.

3. **According to Wiersbe, what are the results of grace?** Grace does not kill us for our sins but gives us the strength to endure the consequences. It frees us to obey the Lord (See Warren Weirsbe, *Be Right (Romans), David C. Cook, 1977.*)

4. **How did Amnon's murder solve a problem for David?** It brought justice to Amnon that the law required, yet David couldn't bring himself to execute. David no longer had to guard Amnon or referee the division between his two sons.

SESSION 15
DAVID'S FLIGHT: CHAPTERS 14:28–33 & 15

CORE QUESTIONS

2 Samuel 14:28

1. Why did Absalom live for two years in Jerusalem without seeing the king? David ignored his son for two years, barring him from his presence and from the privilege of the king's table.

2 Samuel 14:29

2. Why did Absalom send for Joab twice? Absalom wanted answers for why he was still being ostracized. He assumed that Joab would know the answers or at least could get him in to see David.

2 Samuel 14:30

3. How did Absalom get Joab's attention when he refused to respond? Absalom ordered his servants to set Joab's fields on fire.

2 Samuel 14:31–32

4. When Joab responded to the arson, why did Absalom say that he needed to speak with the king? Absalom wanted Joab to ask David why he had brought him from Geshur. He told Joab that he wanted to see the king's face.

2 Samuel 14:33

5. How did David react to Absalom prostrating himself before him? He extended forgiveness and embraced his son.

2 Samuel 15:1

6. What did Absalom provide for himself, and what did they represent? A chariot, horses, and fifty men as runners. This was now the proper way for kings to make an entrance in Israel.

ANSWER KEY

2 Samuel 15:2–6

7. **What did Absalom do to steal away the hearts of the men of Israel?** He rose early to hear the suits that came to the king for judgment. He put doubt in people's minds about David and a bug in their ears to promote him as a judge. He played the political nice guy and won their affections.

2 Samuel 15:7–9

8. **What did Absalom ask permission to do, and what was his supposed purpose?** He asked for permission to travel to Hebron to worship the Lord, as he vowed to do while living at Geshur.

2 Samuel 15:10

9. **What did Absalom do instead of going to the house of the Lord to worship?** He sent spies throughout Israel to announce Absalom as king when they heard the trumpet.

2 Samuel 15:11–12

10. **Whom did Absalom rally to his cause?** Two hundred men who knew nothing of the coup but went with him innocently from Jerusalem. Also, Ahithophel, David's counselor.

2 Samuel 15:13–14

11. **When David heard that the men of Israel were behind Absalom becoming king, what did he do?** David and his servants fled out of fear of Absalom.

2 Samuel 15:15–18

12. **Why was leaving the city the best option for David and his people?** He knew that Absalom's popularity meant David had few allies, and attacking Hebron would likely lead to defeat. He was unwilling to see war destroy the city he built, and if he stayed locked up in the city, they would all appear weak and end up under house arrest.

2 Samuel 15:19–21

13. **What unlikely person followed David, and why?** Ittai, a Gittite from Gath, followed him voluntarily. He had come to the city only the day before, but Ittai told David that he would go wherever the king was, even if it meant death.

2 Samuel 15:22

14. **How did David respond to Ittai?** He told him to go on and pass over with the rest of David's people.

2 Samuel 15:23

15. **Where did their "passing" lead them?** It took them through the Kidron Valley and up the Mount of Olives, eastward out of the city and into the wilderness.

16. **What was the significance of this wilderness?** David knew this place all too well from his years of fleeing from Saul. Once again, it would be the place where David retreated to fight a foe for control of the throne of Israel.

2 Samuel 15:24

17. **What did Zadok and the Levites attempt to carry out of Jerusalem?** They brought out the ark of the covenant of God.

2 Samuel 15:25–26

18. **Why did David command them to return the ark to the city?** He said that if he found favor in the sight of the Lord, then God would bring him back again, and the ark would be in its rightful place in Jerusalem. If God didn't delight in him, then he agreed for God to do whatever He deemed right.

2 Samuel 15:27–28

19. **Why did David tell Zadok to remain in Jerusalem with the ark?** He had Zadok and his family return to serve the Lord and to let David know of any news in Jerusalem while he was in the wilderness.

ANSWER KEY

2 Samuel 15:29–30

20. **In what manner did David leave Jerusalem?** He ascended the Mount of Olives barefoot, with his head covered, weeping.

2 Samuel 15:31

21. **Who did a messenger say was conspiring with Absalom?** His wife's grandfather, Ahithophel.

22. **Why was this man dangerous to David?** He was a former counselor for David and would have known his military forces well.

23. **What did David pray would happen to his counsel?** That his counsel would be foolishness.

2 Samuel 15:32–34

24. **When Hushai the Archite came to the summit to meet David, he turned him back to the city. What command did he give the man?** To return to the city as a spy and pledge allegiance to Absalom.

2 Samuel 15:35–37

25. **To whom was Hushai to report everything, who would then send word to David?** Zadok and Abiathar, the priests.

Discussion Questions (Answers may vary.)

1. **Why did Absalom choose Hebron as the place to announce his coup?** It was the place of David's anointing (2 Samuel 2:1–4; 5:1–3), so there was symbolism in ascending the throne at Hebron. It was a safe distance from Jerusalem so he could prepare for an attack. Absalom was born in Hebron, so he likely intended to make it the capital again.

2. **David recognized that the Lord was bringing discipline upon him by removing him from the city. Why didn't David want the ark of the Lord with him in the wilderness?** He knew that God wanted the ark and the priests to remain in Jerusalem. He accepted the discipline from the Lord, but that didn't mean it was a sign that God was moving the ark or the priesthood.

3. How does David's prayer to turn Ahithophel's counsel into foolishness reveal a heart change in David? When David faced difficult odds, he learned to lean on the Lord and appeal to Him rather than rely on himself. David turned back to prayer and worship.

SESSIONS 16–17
DAVID'S FLIGHT CONTINUED: CHAPTERS 16 & 17

Background

1. By leaving the ark in Jerusalem, against normal patterns of kings, what was David effectively saying about where his power originated from? That the ark was not a symbol of his power or reign. It represented God's reign over Israel.

2. How did David's acknowledgment of God's sovereignty during his exile contribute to subsequent events? David received the Lord's discipline and learned from the experience. David's willingness to follow the Lord created a powerful picture of Jesus doing the Father's will.

CORE QUESTIONS

2 Samuel 16:1–2

3. Mephibosheth's servant, Ziba, met David beyond the summit with gifts of donkeys, bread, raisins, fruit, and wine. Why did Ziba say he was presenting them to David? He said that the supplies were to support the army as they rode out.

2 Samuel 16:3

4. What lie did Ziba tell him about Mephibosheth? He said that Mephibosheth went to Jerusalem, expecting his father's kingdom to result from the infighting.

2 Samuel 16:4

5. How did David respond, which perfectly played into Ziba's plan? He gave all of Mephibosheth's property to Ziba.

ANSWER KEY

2 Samuel 16:5–6

6. **Who came out to David in Bahurim, and what did he do?** Shimei, from the house of Saul, came out, cursing David.

2 Samuel 16:7–8

7. **What curses did Shimei yell at David as he passed by?** He called David a man of bloodshed and worthless. He claimed that David's exile was caused by David killing Saul and his sons.

2 Samuel 16:9–11

8. **Abishai came to David's side and asked for permission to kill Shimei. What was David's response?** He told Abishai to leave him alone. If God had told him to curse David, then they would be fighting against the Lord.

2 Samuel 16:12–13

9. **What was David hoping for in allowing the man to continue cursing him?** That the Lord would see his affliction and return good to him.

2 Samuel 16:14

10. **Where did David and his men hide out while Absalom entered Jerusalem, and for what reason?** They hid in Bahurim to refresh themselves and wait for word from their allies in the kingdom.

2 Samuel 16:15–16

11. **As soon as Absalom entered Jerusalem, what did Hushai do to gain Absalom's trust?** He came to Absalom, saying, "Long live the king!"

2 Samuel 16:17–19

12. **When Absalom questioned why Hushai did not follow David into exile, what was his response?** Hushai told him that he would serve whomever the Lord chose for Israel. He meant David but worded everything in a way that convinced Absalom he was referring to him.

2 Samuel 16:20–22

13. What counsel did Ahithophel first give to Absalom? He told him to sleep with his father's concubines to show symbolically that he was taking over the kingdom.

2 Samuel 16:23

14. What was Ahithophel's authority in both David's and Absalom's courts? His counsel was regarded as equal to the word of God and was never challenged.

2 Samuel 17:1

15. What did Ahithophel ask Absalom's permission to do? To allow him to pick twelve thousand men to go attack David.

2 Samuel 17:2–4

16. How did Ahithophel propose to defeat David? He would attack while David was weary, causing the people to scatter. Then he would kill only David and bring the people back to Jerusalem to serve Absalom.

2 Samuel 17:5–6

17. Why did Absalom invite Hushai to give his opinion on the plan of attack? Absalom intended to trap Hushai to test whether he was still loyal to David. If he were, then he would likely have tried to talk Absalom out of the attack.

2 Samuel 17:7–8

18. What was Hushai's response to Absalom, and why did he say that Ahithophel's advice was not good? He told Absalom that Ahithophel's advice was not good this time. David would not spend the night with the people in the open city since he was an expert in warfare.

2 Samuel 17:9–10

19. Where did Hushai say that David would likely go to spend the night? He insisted that David would be in a cave, out of sight and out of reach.

Answer Key

2 Samuel 17:11–13

20. **What was Hushai's suggested plan of attack for Absalom?** Rather than attack right away, he should gather every man from Dan to Beersheba. Then they would attack David and the men with him. This was to delay the attack and give David time to prepare. If he ran into a city, they would attack the city and tear it to the ground.

2 Samuel 17:14

21. **What was the ultimate reason Absalom listened to Hushai's advice instead of Ahithophel's?** The Lord had frustrated the good advice of Ahithophel to bring disaster upon Absalom.

2 Samuel 17:15–16

22. **To whom did Hushai tell the plan of attack, and what was the purpose?** As soon as Absalom agreed, Hushai told Zadok and the priests what Ahithophel had counseled and then what he had counseled. To allow David time and a better angle for defense, he told them to cross over and not spend the night at the fords of the wilderness.

2 Samuel 17:17

23. **Who were the spies who went to tell David the plans Hushai had relayed through a maidservant?** Jonathan and Ahimaaz.

2 Samuel 17:18–20

24. **After a boy spotted Jonathan and Ahimaaz leaving, he ran and told Absalom. Where did the men hide to avoid capture?** They hid in a well at a man's house in Bahurim. The maidservant covered the opening and put grain on it so it looked undisturbed. She told Absalom's servants that they had crossed the brook.

2 Samuel 17:21–22

25. **What would David's escape inevitably mean for Absalom?** David was the superior military leader. This meant that he would have time to gather troops to fight head-on, which would mean doom for Absalom.

2 Samuel 17:23

26. **Knowing that he had betrayed God's anointed and David's escape would mean his inevitable death, what did Ahithophel do?** He went home, set his house in order, and strangled himself.

2 Samuel 17:24

27. **Where did David go before Absalom crossed the Jordan?** David went to Mahanaim.

Discussion Questions (Answers may vary.)

1. **What four points of comparison exist between David's flight and Christ's departure after His first coming?**
   - David entered Jerusalem to a joyous reception but then was rejected, as was Christ.
   - When David left, he was followed mostly by Gentile supporters. Jesus' church became largely Gentile.
   - When David departed the city, he left by the Mount of Olives, and Jesus ascended to the Father the same way.
   - David ordered that the ark remain in the city, just as Jesus commanded His disciples to await the arrival of the Spirit.

2. **What was David's chief weakness as a leader and king? What was he lacking?** David was too trusting of bad men and lacked discernment to separate truth from falsehood and to recognize the difference between wisdom and foolishness.

3. **Shimei wrongly blamed David for killing Saul and Abner. How did David take his chastisement?** He heard it as the Lord chastising him for killing Uriah, knowing it was right and proper judgment.

4. **What was significant about the location where Absalom chose to take advantage of David's concubines?** It was in a tent on the roof where David stood, spying on Bathsheba.

ANSWER KEY

5. **What lesson for followers of Christ regarding spiritual warfare can be gleaned from Hushai's cunning?** To "be shrewd as serpents and innocent as doves" (Matthew 10:16).

SESSION 18
THE DOWNFALL OF ABSALOM: CHAPTERS 17:24–29; 18; & 19:1–7

CORE QUESTIONS

2 Samuel 17:24

1. **Although the land God gave Israel spanned both east and west of the Jordan River, what did the Jews believe crossing the Jordan meant?** Since Jews stayed to the west of the Jordan, crossing to the east was seen as leaving Israel.

2 Samuel 17:25

2. **Whom did Absalom appoint as commander of his army in place of Joab? What was significant about this choice?** Absalom appointed Amasa, Joab's second cousin. By choosing a man with family ties to David's commander, he reinforced the idea that he was a legitimate replacement king. Amasa was also an Ishmaelite, not an Israelite, (a non-Jew) which showed Absalom's lack of relationship with the God of Israel.

2 Samuel 17:26–29

3. **As Absalom camped in the land of Gilead, what did David's allies bring for his people?** Beds, sheep, food, utensils, and sweet honey.

2 Samuel 18:1–2

4. **How did David divide his fighting men to prepare for battle?** He divided them into thousands and hundreds. He shared the command of these forces among three trusted and competent men: Joab, Abishai, and Ittai.

5. **What was the valiant proposal that David made to his fighting men?** He told them that he would go to battle with them.

2 Samuel 18:3–4

6. What was the people's response to David, and what did they say David was worth? They told him not to go with them, for if they scattered, David would be singled out and killed. They said that he was worth ten thousand of the men and it would be better for him to help them from the city.

2 Samuel 18:5

7. What were David's instructions to his commanders regarding Absalom? He instructed the commanders and all the people not to kill Absalom and to deal gently with him.

2 Samuel 18:6–8

8. What was the outcome of the battle, and how many men died? The people of Israel lost to David's men, and twenty thousand men died.

2 Samuel 18:9

9. How did Absalom become trapped in a tree? He was riding on his mule when it went under the thick branches of a great oak. His head (rather, his hair) became caught in the branches, and the mule kept going.

2 Samuel 18:10–11

10. When a messenger told Joab that he saw Absalom hanging, how did Joab respond? Joab was upset that the soldier didn't use the chance to kill Absalom.

2 Samuel 18:12–13

11. How was the soldier correct in refraining from killing Absalom? He was correctly following David's orders. To raise his hand against the king's son when the king directed otherwise was rebellion. Everyone also likely remembered how David dealt with the man who claimed to have killed Saul, even though Saul was already dying.

ANSWER KEY

2 Samuel 18:14–15

12. **What did Joab do after hearing the soldier's report?** He took three spears and thrust them through Absalom's heart. Then the young men with him followed suit and killed him.

2 Samuel 18:16

13. **Why did Joab call off the pursuit of the Israelite people after Absalom's death?** There was no point in pursuing fellow Israelites once their cause was eliminated.

2 Samuel 18:17–18

14. **How did Joab and the men dispose of Absalom's body?** They buried him under a high pile of stones in the middle of the forest.

15. **What was significant about this burial?** This ensured that Absalom was not buried as a hero or a martyr but in a hidden grave. It's ironic since the penalty for a rebellious son was stoning (Deuteronomy 21:18–21).

2 Samuel 18:19–20

16. **Why did Ahimaaz so desperately want to run and tell David the result of the battle?** Typically, a messenger who brought good news would be rewarded on the spot.

17. **Why did Joab deny him the opportunity to convey the message?** Joab wisely attempted to spare the man, knowing that the news of Absalom's death would not make David happy.

2 Samuel 18:21–23

18. **Whom did Joab appoint to tell the king of his son's death, and why did he choose him?** He appointed a Gentile soldier from Cush to tell David, likely because he was expendable, whereas Joab valued Ahimaaz.

19. **What did Ahimaaz say when he insisted on going with him?** He insisted to Joab that he was willing to face whatever happened, but he still wanted to run to the king.

2 Samuel 18:24–27

20. **Why did David consider the men running by themselves to be good news?** If the news had been bad, there would have been a great retreat of many people running back.

2 Samuel 18:28–30

21. **What news did Ahimaaz bring to David?** He told the king that the battle had been won but lied to him, saying that he knew nothing of Absalom's fate.

22. **Why did Ahimaaz lie to the king?** He wanted to get credit for the good news and leave the bad news for the Cushite to deliver to David.

2 Samuel 18:31–32

23. **How did the Cushite deliver the news of Absalom's death to the king?** He opened with news of the defeat of the rebellion. When David asked of Absalom, he respectfully answered that he wished all the king's enemies would be like that young man.

2 Samuel 18:33

24. **What emotional response did David have to the messengers' reports?** David went up into his chambers and wept for his son.

2 Samuel 19:1–2

25. **What did David's mourning cause the nation to do?** Instead of rejoicing over their victory, they mourned with the king over the loss of his son.

2 Samuel 19:3–4

26. **How did the soldiers return from battle, and how was this different from how they should have returned?** Instead of being happy and proud, they had to return to the city quietly, as humiliated people who had to flee from battle.

Answer Key

2 Samuel 19:5

27. **How did Joab chastise David for his public mourning?** He said that the people were covered in shame because although they fought to save David and his family, David was mourning over their victory.

2 Samuel 19:6

28. **How did Joab wisely describe David's action of mourning?** That it was as if David loved those who hated him and hated those who loved him.

2 Samuel 19:7

29. **What was Joab's final, bold demand to the king?** He told the king that he needed to go out before the people who fought for him and make things right.

Discussion Questions (Answers may vary.)

1. **What are some subtle cues in chapter 18 that reinforce that David, not Absalom, was king?** David was referred to as king to emphasize his rightful place. The story is also constructed as a contrast between David and Absalom so that we see the difference in their hearts.

2. **Why did David's people insist that he stay away from the battle?** At this point, David was an older man, so his value as a leader had changed. Now he was more valuable in the rear ranks, giving orders rather than fighting.

3. **While mercy and kindness are virtues, when do they do more harm than good?** When they become an excuse for overlooking disobedience and rebellion. Just as justice without mercy and kindness hardens the heart, so kindness and mercy without justice become a license to sin.

4. **How was it that more of Absalom's men died in the forest as they were running from the battle than in the battle itself?** The forests of Gilead were overrun with dangers and obstacles, such as horrible rock piles, prickly oaks, and thorns. (See William M. Thomson, "Ladder of Tire-Acre" (ch. 21), in *The Land and the Book*, Harper & Brothers, 1858.)

2 SAMUEL

5. What did David's mourning over Absalom show to the people? That he was more focused on his personal loss than on the nation's gain. The people were embarrassed and changed their victory celebrations into mourning.

SESSION 19
REINSTATED AS KING: CHAPTER 19

Background

1. **How did David's actions in mourning for his son shame his people?** His actions suggested that David valued Absalom, a traitor, more than he valued his loyal men.

2. **Joab's chastisement of David revealed what David had become as a father and a king. What is the basic principle of biblical leadership reflected in David's shortcomings?** That who we are at home in leading our families is who we will be in leading God's people.

CORE QUESTIONS

2 Samuel 19:8

3. **What was David's response to Joab's demands?** He arose and sat in the city gates to commend his people for their victory.

2 Samuel 19:9–10

4. **What were the main points of confusion among the tribes of Israel?** The people were worried about what would come next. Those who sided with Absalom fled to their tents and quarreled over what David would do next. Many thought that David had abdicated the throne by fleeing, so they were unsure about who was in control.

2 Samuel 19:11–12

5. **What were David's intentions in addressing the house of Judah?** He extended an olive branch to his tribe, expecting them to embrace him again as their king.

ANSWER KEY

2 Samuel 19:13

6. Why did David replace Joab with Amasa as commander? Joab had killed Absalom against David's express wishes.

2 Samuel 19:14–15

7. How did Judah respond to David's message? They invited him back to Jerusalem and met him at Gilgal to bring him back across the Jordan.

2 Samuel 19:16–17

8. Who came to meet the king, along with the tribe of Judah? Benjamites of the tribe of Saul, the servant Ziba, with his sons and servants, and Shimei.

2 Samuel 19:18–20

9. Who fell at David's feet, and what was his plea? Shimei, the one who cursed the king, fell before him and begged him not to count him as guilty. He admitted that he had sinned and was the first of the house of Joseph to run out and meet the king.

2 Samuel 19:21

10. Many of those around David objected to the prospect of showing forgiveness. What did Abishai say to the king? He said that Shimei should be put to death for cursing the Lord's anointed.

2 Samuel 19:22–23

11. What was David's Christlike response to Shimei? He told him that there was no reason the house of Shimei should be an adversary to him. He pardoned his sin and swore to him that he would not die for his crime.

2 Samuel 19:24

12. Why did Mephibosheth come out to David in such an unkempt manner? From the time of David's exile, he did not care for himself as a sign of mourning. He showed himself to David in this manner as proof that he had been on David's side the whole time.

2 Samuel 19:25–26

13. When David asked Mephibosheth why he didn't go with him, what was his reason? That Ziba had lied to him and, instead of saddling a donkey for him, had taken it and left Mephibosheth behind.

2 Samuel 19:27–28

14. Mephibosheth told David that Ziba had lied about him, but because he started with nothing, what did he leave to David's wise counsel? Since he had nothing and it was only David's kindness that gave him the rights of a son, even sitting at the king's table, he said that he wouldn't complain and would rely on the king to do what he thought was right.

2 Samuel 19:29

15. Surprisingly, what was David's reaction to discovering Ziba's deception? He dismissed the entire conversation and divided the estate, giving each man half.

2 Samuel 19:30

16. What was Mephibosheth's response to this? What did he want more than anything else? Mephibosheth said that he would let Ziba have everything since David was now back on the throne. All he wanted was for David to be reinstated as king.

2 Samuel 19:31–32

17. Who supported David during his exile? Barzillai the Gileadite. He also escorted David back across the Jordan.

2 Samuel 19:33

18. What kindness did David extend to Barzillai for taking care of him and his men? He offered for the man to cross the Jordan with him, and he would take care of him for the rest of his life.

2 Samuel 19:34–36

19. What were Barzillai's reasons for refusing David's offer? He was eighty years old and could not fully enjoy the luxuries or be of any help in David's court.

ANSWER KEY

2 Samuel 19:37–38

20. What did Barzillai suggest instead that David wholeheartedly agreed to do? To allow his son, Chimham, to cross over with the king and be provided for in the same way David had offered Barzillai.

2 Samuel 19:39–41

21. As David crossed over with the people of Judah and his followers, the other tribes came to greet him. What did they immediately start complaining about? They complained that Judah stole David away, making them look bad for not coming out to support him.

2 Samuel 19:42–43

22. In a comical way, the tribes argued over whose idea it was to bring the king back home. How is this ironic when we consider how David left to go into exile? When he left Jerusalem, he didn't have a single ally except Gentile mercenary soldiers. Now everyone welcomed him home with open arms upon his return.

Discussion Questions (Answers may vary.)

1. **What prophetic picture do we see in the events of David's exile and return?** David's departure from Jerusalem created a picture of Jesus' departure from it at His first coming. David withheld judgment against those who opposed him, knowing that God would appoint the outcome, just as Jesus did.

2. **What four representative families who embrace the return of Jesus are mentioned in Zechariah 12?** David, Nathan, Levi, and Shimei.

3. **Whom does Shimei represent in Jesus' return?** He represents Jesus' enemies, those who opposed Him and drove Him out of Jerusalem at His first coming.

4. **Why was Mephibosheth fine with Ziba having the entirety of his estate?** He had nothing before David's kindness was shown to him, and he knew that as long as he had a friendship with the king, it didn't matter how much he possessed. He could always count on the king to support him and his family.

2 SAMUEL

SESSION 20
SHEBA'S REBELLION: CHAPTER 20

Background

1. **Why did the men of Israel and Judah argue at the banks of the Jordan River, according to 2 Samuel 19?** Since Judah was the first to welcome the king back into Jerusalem, the rest of the tribes felt this demonstrated that Israel had no claim to the king.

2. **What would these arguments eventually lead to in 1 Kings 12?** The separation of Israel and Judah into two kingdoms.

CORE QUESTIONS

2 Samuel 20:1–2

3. **What did Sheba do that drove a wedge further into the division of the people?** He blew the shofar and announced that Israel had no portion in David or any inheritance. He called them to leave David and go back to their tents.

2 Samuel 20:3

4. **What did David do when he first returned to his house?** He got his house in order. He took the concubines who had been raped and set them up to be taken care of for the rest of their lives.

5. **Why was this act significant?** Since they were raped by David's son, meaning that he could not take them back to himself, they would have been abandoned to a lifetime of being alone and uncared for. He made sure that they were taken care of.

2 Samuel 20:4

6. **After David took care of his concubines, what did he summon Amasa, the new commander, to do?** To assemble the men of Judah within three days in Gibeon to take down Sheba.

ANSWER KEY

2 Samuel 20:5–6

7. **When Amasa delayed longer than the appointed time, what was David's follow-up plan?** He sent Abishai, Joab's brother, to take David's personal elite troops to pursue Sheba.

2 Samuel 20:7

8. **David sent Abishai to pursue Sheba, but who went after him? How did the military authority shift when he did?** Joab and his men went out from Jerusalem. Apparently, Joab went along with his brother and took the opportunity to lead. Military power shifted back to Joab.

2 Samuel 20:8

9. **Whom did Joab catch up to in his pursuit of Sheba?** He caught up to Amasa at the great rock in Gibeon.

2 Samuel 20:9–10

10. **What did Joab do as he got close to Amasa?** He grabbed his beard as if to kiss him and then stabbed him in the stomach with his dagger.

2 Samuel 20:11

11. **One of Joab's men stood beside Amasa and made a declaration to the troops. Why was his statement so important?** It was a statement of resolve to weed out those who had secretly sided with Amasa to delay David's mission. Those who were on the side of the king needed to follow Joab, and those who weren't would be killed. It also showed who was then fully in charge of the army.

2 Samuel 20:12

12. **What was the solution for the troops being distracted by Amasa's mangled body?** They dragged him from the road into a field and threw a garment over him.

2 Samuel 20:13–14

13. **How far did the army travel to pursue Sheba in the north?** Approximately ninety miles north and four miles west to a town called Abel.

2 Samuel 20:15

14. What were Joab and his men doing in an attempt to get to Sheba? They cast up a siege ramp against the city, wreaking destruction to topple the wall.

2 Samuel 20:16–17

15. Who requested to speak with Joab, and was this typical for cities to do? A wise woman, likely an elderly delegate who would proctor peace for the city, requested to speak directly to Joab.

2 Samuel 20:18–19

16. What was the woman's appeal to Joab? She told him that the city was one of peace, where they attempted to reconcile before turning to violence.

2 Samuel 20:20–22

17. Was Joab's main purpose in the attack to destroy the city and the inheritance of the Lord? What was his goal? He told the woman that he didn't want to destroy anyone or anything. He only wanted Sheba, as he had lifted his hand against King David.

18. What was the woman's response? Did it appease Joab? She told him that they would throw Sheba's head over the wall to him. Once done, Joab blew the shofar in victory and left the city.

2 Samuel 20:23–26

19. As David's administrators are listed, who is named instead of Abishai as being over the whole army of Israel? Joab was now over the army, likely for his victory and leadership over capturing Sheba.

Discussion Questions (Answers may vary.)

1. Why was blowing the shofar significant when Sheba made his declaration? Blowing the shofar typically either declared war or introduced royalty. In this case, it was a revolt against the rightful king of Israel.

ANSWER KEY

2. Why was David unable to be with his concubines after Absalom's treachery? When Absalom raped David's concubines, it symbolized a transfer of royal power, in this case to an illegitimate successor. Since this act had been committed against them, he could no longer call them his.

3. Why was it crucial for David to get to Sheba as quickly as possible? It was less about Sheba's declaration and more about the potential growth of division between Israel and Judah. David was trying to eliminate the wedge further separating his kingdom.

4. What are two potential reasons Joab killed Amasa? Amasa's failure to accomplish the command of David could have revealed him as a potential rogue commander, showing a lack of loyalty to David. It could also have been simply a jealous response by Joab for his promotion into Joab's post.

SESSION 21
BIBLICAL JUSTICE: CHAPTER 21:1–14

Background

1. How did Sheba sow division between Judah and Israel? He announced to the people that they had no part in the king and for all of Israel to follow him back to their homes.

2. Who was originally in charge of the troops sent to gather the men of Judah before Joab regained control? Amasa was charged with gathering the men of Judah.

CORE QUESTIONS

2 Samuel 21:1

3. What was occurring in the land that caused David to seek the presence of the Lord? There was a severe famine for three years.

4. What did God say was the reason the land was enduring hardship? Saul and his household had put the Gibeonites to death.

2 Samuel

2 Samuel 21:2–3

5. **What did David do to try to rectify the situation?** He called the Gibeonites and asked what he should do for them to make atonement.

2 Samuel 21:4

6. **What did the Gibeonites say they had no desire for regarding restitution?** They did not want any payment (silver or gold) and were in no place to put any Israelite to death.

2 Samuel 21:5–6

7. **What did the people request of the king as payment for Saul's crimes? Which law did the Gibeonites apply in this request?** They requested that seven men from Saul's line be handed over to them to be hanged. This was according to the law in Exodus 21:23–25 that demanded an eye for an eye, tooth for tooth, and life for life.

2 Samuel 21:7

8. **Who among Saul's line did David spare, and why?** He spared Mephibosheth because of the oath of the Lord between David and Jonathan.

2 Samuel 21:8–9

9. **Where were the men from Saul's household put to death? Why was this location significant?** They were executed in Gibeah, where Saul was from.

2 Samuel 21:10

10. **What did Rizpah, Aiah's daughter, do after the men were killed?** She stayed by the bodies to keep the birds and beasts away.

2 Samuel 21:11–12

11. **What did David do in response to Rizpah's actions?** He retrieved the bones of Saul and Jonathan from Jabesh-gilead.

ANSWER KEY

12. **Why were Saul's and Jonathan's bones located in Jabesh-gilead?** The men of Jabesh-gilead had stolen them from the open square of Beth-shan where they had been hanged by the Philistines.

2 Samuel 21:13–14

13. **How was David merciful to Rizpah after Saul and Jonathan's bones were gathered?** He gathered them together with the bodies of the men who were killed and buried them in Benjamin in the family grave.

14. **What was God's response to this act of justice and mercy?** He was moved by prayer for the land.

Discussion Questions (Answers may vary.)

1. **How was a covenant established between Israel and the Gibeonites (Joshua 9)?** Joshua and the men of Israel were tricked by the men of Gibeon, causing them to believe that they were foreigners to be protected. Instead, they were neighbors who simply did not want to be among the ones slaughtered.

2. **Why did Joshua fall for the Gibeonites' trickery?** He had not sought the counsel of the Lord regarding the situation.

3. **Why did David need to make atonement for the Gibeonites?** Saul broke the covenant formed between Israel and the Gibeonites, and no restitution had been made.

4. **Why did Rizpah remain with the hung bodies?** She knew that the law required the honor of burial. She was also displaying her desperation as a mother to protect her sons, out of love.

SESSION 22A
"THE HORN OF MY SALVATION": CHAPTERS 21:15–22 & 22:1–20

CORE QUESTIONS

2 Samuel 21:15

1. **What does "David became weary" mean in this text?** The Hebrew uses this to mean that he either had fainted or was losing consciousness. (See *Strong's Concordance*, "H5774 – ûp.")

2. **How was the enemy in this battle reminiscent of Goliath, whom David fought in his youth?** Ishbi-benob was a Philistine from among the descendants of the giant, just as Goliath was.

2 Samuel 21:17

3. **Who helped David and struck down the giant? What did he tell David?** Abishai helped David and killed the Philistine. He told David not to go out with them into battle again so that he would not extinguish the lamp of Israel.

2 Samuel 21:18–22

4. **Time and again, David and his men defeated the Philistines and the giants among them. How did God demonstrate His power through weakness in David's battles?** When David was faint, God protected him from being killed. All through the battles, whether due to numbers or size, God was mighty through His seemingly weaker people.

2 Samuel 22:1–2

5. **When did David speak or sing the song recorded here?** On the day the Lord saved David from the hand of all his enemies and from the hand of Saul.

2 Samuel 22:3–4

6. **From what did David credit God for saving him?** From the constant external and internal attacks within Israel toward David.

ANSWER KEY

2 Samuel 22:5–6

7. **What four things did David say were scaring or ensnaring him?** The waves of death, the floods of destruction, the ropes of Sheol, and the snares of death.

2 Samuel 22:7

8. **What did David do in his distress, and what was God's response?** He called upon the Lord, and He heard David's voice.

2 Samuel 22:8–9

9. **How was the earth affected by the Lord's anger?** The earth shook, the foundations of heaven trembled and were shaken, smoke went up from His nostrils, and fire came from His mouth.

2 Samuel 22:10–11

10. **How did the Lord come down from heaven?** He came down from the heavens with thick darkness under His feet. He rode on a cherub and appeared on the wings of the wind.

2 Samuel 22:12–14

11. **What elements of nature did David use to describe the Lord's descent from heaven?** Darkness, thick clouds, and a mass of water, fire, and thunder.

2 Samuel 22:15–16

12. **What did the Lord use to scatter David's enemies?** Arrows from heaven.

13. **What natural effects did the Lord's rebuke have on the world?** Channels of the sea appeared, and the foundations of the world were laid bare.

2 Samuel 22:17–18

14. **How did the Lord rescue David after rebuking his enemies?** He drew David out of many waters and delivered him from his strong enemy.

2 Samuel

2 Samuel 22:19–20

15. What did David say was the reason the Lord rescued him? The Lord delighted in him.

Discussion Questions (Answers may vary.)

1. Why was David told not to go into battle anymore? Due to his becoming faint, it was too much of a risk for him to go into battle. His life was too precious to lose.

2. In the first few verses of 2 Samuel 22, how can we see that David had an intimate relationship with God? The use of the word "my" in reference to Yahweh in times of great distress and trouble.

3. In verse 6, to what does the word *Sheol* refer? In this context, it can mean death.

4. How does Jonah's prayer in Jonah 2 compare to David's song of the Lord's deliverance? He called out in his distress, and the Lord heard his voice and answered him.

5. The Lord rescued David because the Lord delighted in him (2 Samuel 22:20). What does the word *delighted* mean in the original language of the text? The word "delighted" is *ha-pes*, meaning to be pleased with or favorable toward. (See *Strong's Concordance*, "H2654 – châphêts")

Session 22B
David's Praise to the Lord: Chapter 22:20–51

Core Questions

2 Samuel 22:21–22

1. For what did David say the Lord rewarded him? For his righteousness and cleanness of hands, for keeping the ways of the Lord and not acting wickedly against God.

ANSWER KEY

2 Samuel 22:23–25

2. **How was David made righteous and clean before a Holy God, even with his sinful acts and mistakes?** David had been awarded righteousness or deemed righteous because he set himself to do the word of God.

3. **Who else in the Old Testament was deemed righteous based on his belief? How was he granted righteousness?** God granted Abraham righteousness based solely on his belief in the Lord (Genesis 15:4–6).

2 Samuel 22:26–27

4. **What concept of holy reciprocity did David attribute to God?** Those in Christ have an Advocate with the Father. We find a response in Christ according to our faithfulness.

5. **How is this same reciprocity seen in reverse for those who are not believers?** The Lord responds to the haughty, the perverted, and the evil according to their ways when they reject His law.

2 Samuel 22:28

6. **Whom does the Lord rescue? Whom is He against?** He rescues those who are afflicted, and He humbles the proud.

2 Samuel 22:29–30

7. **What help did the Lord provide to David?** He shone forth the direction in which David should go. He provided the strength and ability necessary to be victorious over his enemies.

2 Samuel 22:31–32

8. **On what attribute of God did David focus in these verses?** The Lord's blameless and faultless ways that have proven true throughout history.

2 Samuel 22:33

9. **How is one seen as blameless before God? Whose efforts achieve this righteousness?** The blameless position before God is not based on human effort but on the Lord, who has made those who trust in Him righteous.

2 Samuel 22:34–35

10. **How did the Lord prepare David to win against his enemies?** He made him quick and strong. God also set him up in high places so he had power and authority.

2 Samuel 22:36–37

11. **What measures of protection did the Lord give to David throughout his life?** The Lord provided David with a shield of salvation as protection and personally helped him at every turn.

2 Samuel 22:38–39

12. **What did the Lord's help and provisions allow David to do?** David pursued his enemies and destroyed them.

2 Samuel 22:40–41

13. **Although David was mighty in battle, to whom did David attribute his victories?** He said that the Lord made him strong and subdued his enemies under him.

2 Samuel 22:42–43

14. **What happened when David's enemies turned to the Lord for help?** David's enemies had nowhere to turn for help, and he crushed them in victory.

2 Samuel 22:44

15. **Aside from his enemies, what else did David say the Lord delivered him from? How did this secure his kingship?** The Lord delivered him from the contentions of his own people. This allowed him to maintain his headship over the nations.

ANSWER KEY

2 Samuel 22:45–46

16. **How did David's partnership with the Lord garner mercy from surrounding nations?** Foreigners would feign loyalty and obedience to avoid bloodshed.

2 Samuel 22:47–49

17. **What was David ultimately saying when he proclaimed that the Lord lives?** That God is not dead or uninvolved in the affairs of His creation. He is intimately intertwined in the lives of His creation.

2 Samuel 22:50–51

18. **Where and to whom did David announce his praises to the Lord?** David's adoration of the Lord was both public and private, and he declared that he would announce his praises among all the nations.

Discussion Questions (Answers may vary.)

1. **In the Old Testament, salvation is connected to physical deliverance, whereas salvation in the New Testament is connected to spiritual deliverance (eternal security). How does Scripture interlink the outworking of salvation for both the Old and New Testament?** Faith in God's Word / promises.

2. **David was deemed righteous because he trusted in the Lord's promises. How does Scripture define the New Testament believer as being deemed righteous?** Faith in Christ and His finished work.

3. **How does allowing the Lord to fight our battles give greater satisfaction than retaliation does?** It causes us to maintain our integrity before the Lord.

4. **What protection is attributed to David that also shows itself in Ephesians 6?** The shield of faith.

2 SAMUEL

SESSION 23A
DAVID'S LAST SONG: CHAPTER 23:1–7

CORE QUESTIONS

2 Samuel 23:1

1. **Since these were not David's final words before death, what should we understand "last words" to mean in this text?** It is David's final song, his final literary legacy to Israel.

2. **What four descriptors did the poet list in this verse, and at first, to whom do they seem to apply?** "The son of Jesse," "the man who was raised on high," "the anointed of the God of Jacob," and "the sweet psalmist of Israel." They all seem, at first, to apply to David himself.

3. **Based on variations of translation in this verse alone, who is more likely the subject of David's final song to Israel?** The Anointed (Messiah) of the God of Jacob.

2 Samuel 23:2

4. **Who did David say communicated through him to give an understanding of the future Messiah?** The Spirit of the Lord.

2 Samuel 23:3–4

5. **What did David say was the result of one ruling over people in righteousness?** He is like the light of morning at sunrise. He will radiate God's divine glory and will be a blessing to all who come under Him.

2 Samuel 23:5

6. **What is David's first point regarding his household, based on further examination of other translations?** That his household did not deserve the promise because of his failure to rule righteously.

7. **With the proper Hebrew phrasing in translation, what does verse 5 say regarding God's promise?** That God had not *yet* made it grow. David had not yet seen

310

this promise fulfilled, yet he was hopeful that since God said it, He would bring it to fruition.

2 Samuel 23:6

8. **What did David say will happen to the "worthless," or evil?** The ones who reject the King will be thrust away like thorns.

2 Samuel 23:7

9. **What were David's intentions in focusing on those who rejected the King?** He was drawing a line in the sand, telling the people that they should choose the righteous King and not their own ways. He was warning that rejection of the King would lead to death and judgment by fire.

Discussion Questions (Answers may vary.)

1. **What are the three main reasons for studying the Scriptures?**

    - To grow in knowing more about our Savior, Jesus Christ.
    - To be conformed to Christ's image.
    - To understand God's redemptive plan regarding all things.

2. **How does Acts 2 compare David and Christ regarding their deaths?** David died and was buried, while Christ was resurrected and never saw decay.

3. **What are two requirements for an ideal king to rule in accordance with God's will?** He would rule righteously, and the reason for his upright rule would be his obedience of, submission to, and fear of the Lord.

4. **What four promises did the Lord tell David regarding his seed who would rule on his throne?**

    - He would be an eternal descendant.
    - He would have an eternal kingdom.
    - He would rule on an eternal throne.
    - He would have an eternal house.

SESSION 23B
THE REWARD OF GREAT MEN: CHAPTER 23:8–39

Background

1. **To whom was David referring as the ideal King of Israel?** The Messiah, Jesus Christ.

2. **What will the future King do once and for all?** He will rule mightily, with wisdom and righteousness, and finally do away with wicked men and women and kingdoms.

CORE QUESTIONS

2 Samuel 23:8

3. **According to the ranking of David's men, who was "chief" of the three?** Josheb-basshebeth, a Tahchemonite, was chief of the captains.

4. **How many was David's chief captain said to have killed at once?** Eight hundred men.

2 Samuel 23:9–10

5. **What notable achievement did Eleazar accomplish to earn him the rank of second among David's three mighty men?** He struck the Philistines down with such a great victory that the Israelites only returned after him to strip the slain.

6. **What was significant about the fact that Eleazar fought with David against the Philistines?** He remained with David even when the men of Israel withdrew.

2 Samuel 23:11–12

7. **Why was the plot of land Shammah defended specifically mentioned?** The Philistines were occupying a plot of land that, according to the promise of the Lord, belonged to Israel.

8. **Why was this a demonstration of Shammah's great faith?** It took great faith to believe the Lord's promise in the Torah. God had given the land to Israel, and Shammah fought to defend that promise.

ANSWER KEY

2 Samuel 23:13–14

9. **What other time in David's life was he in the cave of Adullam?** During his escape from King Saul.

2 Samuel 23:15

10. **What was significant about David's craving?** It's likely that David was reminiscing on the fresh taste of water from that well. It was a nostalgic moment of remembering his days as a shepherd in Bethlehem.

2 Samuel 23:16

11. **What did the three mighty men do for David? What risk did they take?** They broke through the Philistine camp and drew water from the well David mentioned. This could have cost them their lives had they been captured.

2 Samuel 23:17

12. **What shocking response did David give in the face of their bravery and loyalty?** He refused to drink the water, recognizing the extreme risk the men took to retrieve it.

2 Samuel 23:18–19

13. **What did it mean that Abishai "had a name" along with the three?** Abishai had earned his reputation in his own right and could hold his own.

2 Samuel 23:20

14. **What was the significance of Benaiah killing a lion in the middle of a pit on a snowy day?** The season and weather conditions—cold, wet, and snowy—speak of this man's strength and impressive record.

2 Samuel 23:21

15. **Who else did Benaiah kill, and how?** Armed with only a club, Benaiah killed an impressive Egyptian with his own spear.

2 SAMUEL

2 Samuel 23:22–23

16. **How did David honor Benaiah?** He appointed him over his guard.

2 Samuel 23:24–39

17. **Why was Joab not mentioned among David's mighty men, even with Joab's many victories?** The men listed as David's mighty men were faithful and obedient. Joab was neither. He played by his own set of rules and did not faithfully obey the king's commands.

Discussion Questions (Answers may vary.)

1. **As believers, when do we receive our rewards?** We receive our rewards when we stand and persevere under trial.

2. **What did David mean in 2 Samuel 23:17 when he said, "Shall I drink the blood of the men who went in jeopardy of their lives?"** David didn't deem himself worthy to drink the water because of the risk these men took on his behalf to obtain it. They could have been killed.

3. **What story in Mark's Gospel is reminiscent of the pouring out of the water in light of a great potential sacrifice?** The story of the unnamed woman who poured out extravagant perfume on Jesus' body.

4. **After salvation, what is the next step for a believer in Christ?** To learn to live and walk obediently in Him.

SESSION 24
SIN, JUDGMENT, AND RESTORATION: CHAPTER 24

CORE QUESTIONS

2 Samuel 24:1

1. **Who incited David to number the people of Israel? Why?** Satan was allowed to incite David to bring about God's plan for bringing judgment on David.

ANSWER KEY

2 Samuel 24:2

2. **What was the root behind God's anger against Israel?** David's arrogance and pride regarding how large his people were in number.

3. **What kind of census was this, since David did not command the women and children to be counted?** It was a military census to show the might of the nation.

2 Samuel 24:3

4. **In response to David's command, what did Joab say the Lord was able to do?** He would add a hundred times as many people if the need arose.

2 Samuel 24:4–8

5. **How long did it take Joab and his men to complete the census?** Nine months and twenty days.

2 Samuel 24:9

6. **How many fighting men were found in Israel and Judah?** Eight hundred thousand men in Israel and five hundred thousand in Judah.

2 Samuel 24:10

7. **Why was David's heart troubled after he numbered the people?** He knew that he had sinned against the Lord by being prideful of and relying on the strength of his numbers instead of the Lord's provision.

8. **What did David immediately do after he recognized his sin?** He prayed to the Lord for forgiveness.

2 Samuel 24:11–12

9. **What did the Lord offer David through his court seer?** He offered David options for discipline and told him to choose.

2 Samuel 24:13

10. **What were David's options for punishment?** Seven years of famine, fleeing for three months before his enemies while they pursued him, or three days of pestilence in the land.

2 Samuel 24:14

11. **What was David's choice for punishment, and what was his reasoning?** He chose the three days of pestilence as he would rather be subject to the hand of God than the hand of men.

2 Samuel 24:15

12. **How many men died as a result of David's sin?** Seventy thousand men.

2 Samuel 24:16

13. **How did the Lord demonstrate His control over the pestilence?** The Lord stopped the hand of the destroying angel when it was time to relent.

14. **What was significant about the location where the angel of destruction stopped?** It was the threshing floor of Araunah the Jebusite (1 Chronicles 21:18–19). This was north of the northern walls of Jerusalem and was not owned by David. It was the location of the Temple Mount and the future site of Solomon's Temple (2 Chronicles 3:1). It's also where Abraham was sent to sacrifice his son, Isaac (Genesis 22:2).

2 Samuel 24:17

15. **What was David's response to the pestilence? Who did he say should be punished?** He cried out for the people, saying that it was he who sinned, not them. He asked for the punishment to be on him and his house.

16. **What caused the Lord to relent?** David repented and took responsibility, bearing the punishment instead of it being on Israel.

Answer Key

2 Samuel 24:18–19

17. What did the prophet tell David to do after his repentance, and where was he to build? He was to build an altar to the Lord on the threshing floor of Araunah the Jebusite.

2 Samuel 24:20

18. What did Araunah do when he saw the king coming toward him? He bowed down with his face to the ground in reverence.

2 Samuel 24:21

19. What did David tell Araunah he wanted to do, and for what purpose? David wanted to buy the threshing floor from him to build an altar to the Lord.

2 Samuel 24:22–23

20. What did Araunah offer the king, free of charge? He offered the land, the animals necessary, and the equipment needed to prepare the altar for sacrifices.

2 Samuel 24:24

21. What was the main reason David insisted on paying for the threshing floor? In a beautiful response to something of such great cost, he refused to offer burnt offerings to the Lord without it costing him anything.

2 Samuel 24:25

22. After David built an altar and offered sacrifices to the Lord, how did the Lord respond? He was moved by the prayers for the land and held back the plague.

Discussion Questions (Answers may vary.)

1. **Why did David believe it was better to endure pestilence than war as a punishment from God?** He knew that the Lord would not cause those who are His to suffer forever. While He is just, He is also a merciful God.

2. **Why did the Lord "relent" and stop the pestilence? Was David able to change God's mind?** God does not change His word or sovereign decree; rather, He

changes how He carries out His judgment according to man's change in conduct. David repented and wanted to bear the burden of punishment instead of his innocent people. He built an altar to the Lord, and this all served to soften God's heart.

3. **Why did Araunah say to David, "May the Lord your God accept you" (2 Samuel 24:23)?** He knew the significance of the sacrifices, that they were to make atonement for sin. He also knew that the pestilence was due to the king being out of fellowship with the Lord.

About the Authors

Stephen Armstrong

Founder of Verse By Verse Ministry International

Stephen Armstrong was the founder and principal teacher of Verse By Verse Ministry International. He came to know the Lord in his early thirties while serving as an Air Force officer. After becoming a believer, Stephen experienced God's call to learn and teach the Bible, so in 1997, Stephen left the military, found a job in Colorado, and began a self-directed course of study in preparation for teaching the Scriptures.

As he devoted himself to study, Stephen developed a love for an in-depth, verse-by-verse style of teaching God's word, believing it to be the best means to persuade the unbeliever of the truth of the gospel and equip the saints for the work of ministry (Romans 10:17; Ephesians 4:14–15).

In 2001, Stephen received God's call to move to San Antonio, Texas, where he soon found opportunities to teach and preach in churches throughout the area. Despite having no professional religious training, in 2003, Stephen was called by God to lead a church-planting effort in the city as pastor of Living Word Fellowship.

That same year, he founded Verse By Verse Ministry of San Antonio (later renamed Verse By Verse Ministry International) out of a desire to offer his unique style of in-depth Bible teaching for free to a worldwide audience. Stephen helped plant Verse By Verse

Fellowship in San Antonio, Texas, in 2018.

Stephen passed away in January 2021, leaving behind a library of insightful Bible teachings and a ministry team committed to advancing the gospel worldwide.

Wesley Livingston

Wesley J. Livingston is the principal Bible teacher of Verse By Verse Ministry International. He lives in San Antonio, Texas, with his wife and two children.

Wesley was drawn to the Lord at an early age through the prayer and dedication of his Christian parents. As a young child, Wesley felt the Lord calling him to ministry. At the age of eighteen, Wesley preached his first sermon. It was then that Wesley knew he was blessed with the gift of teaching.

Wesley attended Prairie View A&M University, where he graduated with bachelor's and master's degrees in architecture. After graduating, he worked at Kirksey Architecture in Houston, Texas, where he was involved in designing science and technology facilities for both private and public organizations. He also taught architecture at the high school level.

After moving to San Antonio, Wesley and his family sought a church that focused on expository Bible teaching. They attended Verse By Verse Fellowship under the leadership and teaching of Pastor Stephen Armstrong. Wesley's desire to teach the Bible grew. In 2020, Wesley began serving as the youth pastor at Verse By Verse Fellowship. Pastor Armstrong personally discipled Wesley to help him grow in his understanding of how to study Scripture and how to deliver God's word through expository teaching. Wesley is committed to the daily study of God's written word.

About Renown Publishing

Renown Publishing is an elite team of professionals devoted to helping you shape, write, and share your book. Renown has written, edited, and worked on hundreds of books (including New York Times, Wall Street Journal, and USA Today best-sellers, and the #1 book on all of Amazon).

We believe authentic stories are the torch of change-makers, and our mission is to collaborate with purpose-driven authors to create societal impact and redeem culture.

If you're the founder of a purpose-driven company, or an aspiring author, visit RenownPublishing.com.

www.ingramcontent.com/pod-product-compliance
Lightning Source LLC
Chambersburg PA
CBHW081203170426
43197CB00018B/2902